Dedication

To Susan,
my wife of thirty years
and partner in adventure.

And to all those who seek
to reunite two exclusive realms:
the Christian life, trusting in Jesus,
and the Jewish life, Yeshua's life,
a life according to Torah.

אי – עוד לא אהבתי די
הרוח והשמש על פני
אי – עוד לא אמרתי די
ואם לא, אם לא עכשיו – אימתי?

Ay – I haven't yet loved enough
The wind and the sun on my face.
Ay – I haven't yet said enough
And if not, if not now – when?

Naomi Shemer

Torah! Torah! Torah!

All Bible quotations are from the KJV.
Torah has been substituted by the author
when the Hebrew of the Tenach is תּוֹרָה *Torah*.
For quotes from the New Covenant, **Torah**
is substituted in most cases when
the passage implies Torah.
Strong's Concordance
is freely quoted.

ISBN: 978-0-692-46688-9

Printed in the United States of America
Published by Hebrew World, Inc.
www.hebrewworld.com
Scottsdale, Arizona

Acknowledgements

Randy, my college roommate, had a Bible calendar open to Joseph revealing himself to his brothers. Randy was Jewish and I was Catholic, but neither of us could explain Joseph. Joseph's identity was hidden from his brothers and from us. We started seeking. Randy found Torah. After a few dead ends, I asked Jesus into my heart. I haven't looked back.

Susan and I met at Bible College. We loved raising our family on rural Vashon Island. Susan educates our children at home and trains them in character. Her description is found on page 70. Josiah, the first sign of my strength, calls our home "a loving boot camp." And Susan conceived this book's title.

Josiah, Nathanael, Adam, and Hosanna grew up learning the Bible from Pastor Frank Davis, who showed us that Israel had the Gospel centuries before Jesus' ministry.

Later, with Hosanna, Savannah, and Kellan, we drank from a fire hose of Torah discovery with Mark Biltz.   Many Torah treasures can be found at www.elshaddaiministries.us and *Blood Moons: Decoding the Imminent Heavenly Signs*, Pastor Mark's recent book. Thanks to Vicki Biltz for her cover photo of Leviticus 10.13-16, the middle words of Torah.

To Hope Egan and D. Thomas Lancaster for *Holy Cow!* and to Daniel Gruber for *Copernicus and the Jews*, thanks for a new perspective. Thanks to Dr. Jeff Larson for critical improvements in content and design. Thanks to Jeff Hancock and Scott Dakers for inspiration. Thanks to Lee Kimzey for objective observations. Thanks to Dr. Danny Ben Gigi for encouragement, his *Hebrew-English Phonetic Bible*, and his newest publication, *Biblical Hebrew Home Study*.

Special thanks to my Dad, Robert Lawson Thalhofer, who always encouraged me to act on my faith, and veteran author of *Company A! Combat Engineers Remember World War II*.

And special thanks to my Mom, Joan Kerwin Thalhofer Z"L, who prayed, and God answered.

Contents

Introduction

"The church's one foundation is Jesus Christ her Lord" begins a hymn which, with centuries of tradition from seminaries and pulpits, helps the church forget its foundation. *Yeshua* (God is Salvation) is *Living Torah,* the Word of God made flesh.[1] Yeshua perfected *Written Torah,* Moses' first five books of the Bible. Replacement Theology morphed this Torah-observant Jewish Messiah into a Torah-breaking Gentile Jesus Christ, rejected Israel, and crushed Jews to create a Gentile church. This shift to Replacement Theology is first seen when *Diotrephes* (Foster Child of Zeus) snubbed the apostle John and rejected Jews.[2] It continued through centuries of violence against Jews and raged during Hitler's Holocaust. Today it bares its teeth whenever the church demonizes Israel, the last stand on earth for Jews. If you pilot a plane, you follow a flight plan. You can't afford to get disoriented. You monitor altitude, attitude, airspeed, heading, and course deviation by watching the instruments. The church ignored its own Instruments and soon lost its way. By God's Grace, the right data is still accessible.

Growing up Catholic, then asking Jesus into my heart as a Protestant, I thought the Gospel began with the church. Jesus fulfilled Torah so that we don't have to. Torah was abolished, but Jews still sought righteousness under Law. I learned the term "invincible ignorance." Jews were smart, but somehow they missed Jesus and how He replaced Law with Grace.

Decades later, our family learned the Bible's definition of the New Covenant: Torah written in the heart. We took off on an adventure. We discovered a worldwide community of believers who are leaving unbiblical traditions. The church says that seeking Torah is trying to earn salvation. But that straw man isn't true of Jews[3] or believers in Yeshua, *Living Torah Who showed us how to keep Written Torah.* When the church rejected its own foundation of Written and Living Torah, it went off-course. Climb aboard now and join us as we return to the church's original flight plan. We are seeking both Written Torah and the true Living Torah, Yeshua.

Tradition over Torah

Many new believers love to read the Word of God. They see that the Bible commands a seventh-day Sabbath.[4] If they ask around, they learn that the early church moved toward a Sunday Sabbath.[5] Catholic Emperor Constantine, when he legalized Christianity, wanted to welcome pagans who already worshipped the sun god on that day.[6] And Jesus rose from the dead on the first day. So that's why the Sabbath is now Sunday, they're told. Traditions which contradict Torah seem to make sense. And everybody does it, so why not? But when the church had the audacity to break the perpetual covenant of Sabbath between God and His people,[7] it earned its own invincible ignorance. The church put tradition over Torah.

Luther's *Ninety-Five Theses*

Catholic priest Johann Tetzel sold indulgences in Europe in the early 1500s. His customers believed that if they bought an indulgence for a departed loved one, no further penance was necessary for the deceased to escape suffering in purgatory. When Tetzel described the agony that could be avoided by a gift of gold, many responded. A couplet is attributed to Tetzel:

> As soon as the gold in the casket rings,
> The rescued soul to heaven springs.[8]

Another Catholic priest, Martin Luther, became enraged at this practice of indulgences. He wrote *The Ninety-Five Theses*, short arguments for Scripture over tradition. Luther rephrased Tetzel for his Thesis 27: "They preach only human doctrines who say that as soon as the money clinks into the money chest, the soul flies out of purgatory."[9] When Luther nailed his *Ninety-Five Theses* to the door of the Castle Church of Wittenberg on October 31st, 1517, he ignited the Protestant Reformation. Later he wrote, "This means that the Word of God—and no one else, not even an angel—should establish articles of faith."[10] *Sola Scriptura* Scripture Alone became a Protestant principle of faith.

Ignoring the Instruments

Yet Luther, like Constantine 1,200 years earlier, rejected Torah. In *How Christians Should Regard Moses* he wrote,

> We will not have Moses as ruler or lawgiver any longer. Indeed God himself will not have it either. Moses was an intermediary soul for the Jewish people. It was to them that he gave the law. We must therefore silence the mouths of those factious spirits who say, "Thus says Moses," etc. Here you simply reply: Moses has nothing to do with us…Moses is dead. His rule ended when Christ came. He is of no further service.[11]

The Catholic who says, "We wrote the Bible, and we're still writing it," and the Protestant who says, "Torah is done away with," represent unbiblical traditions: "God finally gave up on rebellious Israel and Torah wasn't cutting it, so God replaced Israel with the church and Law with Grace." But course deviation is easily corrected with a Bible and a Strong's Concordance. These are two of the Instruments required to get the church back on its original heading.

DNA of the New Covenant

The New Covenant is defined in Hebrews 8.8-12, which quotes Jeremiah 31.31-34. Jeremiah 31.31 is *the only verse in the entire Tenach*, what the church calls the Old Testament, which contains both the words "new" and "covenant." The New Covenant is with **Israel**, not "the church." It is תּוֹרָה *Torah* **written in the heart**. It is **forgiveness of sin,** the only part most of the church knows. Torah can't be "done away with" if it's supposed to be written in our hearts!

The church accepts only the third element, *forgiveness*. But God and His Word remain unchanged. Israel was saved at Passover, baptized into Moses in the Red Sea,[12] and taught Torah at Mt. Sinai. It's the same today. Salvation is by Grace through faith in Yeshua, Israel's Passover Lamb. We are baptized into Living Torah. We follow His Written Torah.

We Need a New Perspective

Daniel Gruber in *Copernicus and the Jews* compares the church's need for a new perspective on Israel and Torah to the days of Copernicus. Everyone knew the universe revolved around the earth—every day the sun came up in the east and set in the west; every year the stars made a circuit in the sky. But why did the planets wander? Scientists devised elaborate theories to explain the planets' strange behavior. Copernicus showed that the planets actually revolve around the sun and don't wander at all. He was called a lunatic. But he was right. The experts were wrong.

After the Temple's destruction in 70 AD and Israel's devastation in 132 AD, Rome branded Israel "Palestine" after Israel's enemies the Philistines. Soon the church declared that it had inherited Torah's blessings, but Israel would keep the curses.   For most of the last 2,000 years, it seemed the church was correct. In 1869, Mark Twain described Israel:

> We traversed some miles of desolate country whose soil is rich enough, but is given over wholly to weeds—a silent, mournful expanse…Gray lizards, those heirs of ruin, of sepulchers and desolation, glided in and out among the rocks…Palestine is desolate and unlovely. And why should it be otherwise? Can the *curse* of the Deity beautify a land? Palestine is no more of this work-day world. It is sacred to poetry and tradition—it is dream-land.[13]

As theologians devise elaborate theories to explain why Israel and Torah have passed away, Israel outlasts all who try to destroy it, just as God promised the prophet Jeremiah,[14] and Torah outlasts heaven and earth, just as Yeshua promised.[15] Right now—*in our lifetime!*—we get to see ancient prophecies fulfilled as Israel returns to its heritage: cities prosper, the desert blooms, and its army is formidable.[16]   To get this new perspective, just hop on an El Al flight. Meet the people. Explore the Israel Mark Twain never saw. See for yourself. The experts are wrong.

Replacement Theology: √ Rejected

God was so angry over the Golden Calf that he planned to destroy Israel and to raise up a new nation through Moses. But Moses rejected this God-given offer of Replacement Theology and begged God to save Israel. God repented![17]

Replacement Theology: √ Accepted

Unlike Moses, the church readily accepted Israel's "rejection." Emperor Constantine said,

> Let us then have nothing in common with the detestable Jewish crowd; for we have received from our Saviour a different way… Beloved brethren, let us with one consent adopt this course, and withdraw ourselves from all participation in their baseness… For how should they be capable of forming a sound judgment, who, since their parricidal guilt in slaying their Lord, have been subject to the direction, not of reason, but of ungoverned passion, and are swayed by every impulse of the mad spirit that is in them?[18]

Julius Streicher, executed Nazi war criminal, said at his trial,

> DR. MARX: Apart from your weekly journal, and particularly after the Party came into power, were there any other publications in Germany which treated the Jewish question in an anti-Semitic way?

> STREICHER: Anti-Semitic publications have existed in Germany for centuries. A book I had, written by Dr. Martin Luther, was, for instance, confiscated. Dr. Martin Luther would very probably sit in my place in the defendants' dock today, if this book had been taken into consideration by the Prosecution. In the book *The Jews and Their Lies,* Dr. Martin Luther writes that the Jews are a serpent's brood and one should burn down their synagogues and destroy them…[19]

Known to Jews, but unknown in the church, Hitler was acting on Luther's advice.[20,21] John Toland, author of the definitive biography *Adolph Hitler,* says that Hitler was a Christian, carrying within him the church's teaching toward Jews.[22]

Luther's rants are downplayed by the church. "Luther was at the end of his life and mentally ill." But this is a double standard since both excuses could be given for Hitler, yet Hitler is rightly held responsible for everything he did. Luther voiced the church's hatred of Israel; Hitler tried to fulfill it. Ironically, German diplomat and Nazi Party member Martin Luther was present at the Wannsee Conference of 1942, where plans for the Final Solution were arranged.

Our Torah Alarm

If a homeowner installs an alarm, who is the most likely to disconnect it—a policeman or a burglar? Our Torah alarm defines a false prophet as one who turns others away from God or His commandments.[23] Who is the most likely to disconnect it—a minister of God or a false prophet? Believers who discover Torah often object concerning the years their Torah alarm was turned off, "We were robbed!"

The Bereans were "more noble"[24] because they tested everything Paul said by searching Torah and Tenach. Since then, the church has done *the exact opposite:* it tests everything in Torah by Paul! Twice in Revelation, the saints are described as those who keep both the commandments of God *and* the faith of Yeshua.[25] Jews seek Written Torah. The church seeks Living Torah. The Bible says to seek both.

My Dad was in France in WWII, driving a jeep full of soldiers. A bullet crashed through the windshield. His commander thought it was friendly fire and ordered my Dad to stop. But Dad hit the gas. The next bullet missed my Dad and killed a man in back. The Nisei, Japanese-American soldiers fighting in Europe, hunted down and killed or captured everyone in that Nazi detachment. My Dad says that the Nazis were terrified of the Nisei, but American soldiers loved having the Nisei on patrol. The Nisei protected their fellow Americans.

Like the Nisei, Torah is a blessing to those who welcome it or a curse to those who fight it, Deuteronomy 11.26-28. In Yeshua, we are freed to welcome Torah because Yeshua took Torah's curse to the grave for us and only Yeshua rose again! That leaves us with Torah's blessings. Torah is our Instrument. Torah is our alarm that warns of false prophets. Even when those false prophets are in the church.

Seek, Seek

Noah sent out a *dove* from the ark. The third time the dove left the ark, it never returned. Where did the dove find יְשׁוּעָה *yeshua* salvation from the flood? 3,000 years after Noah, the Holy Spirit descended *like a dove* and rested on יְשׁוּעַ *Yeshua* as He arose from the waters of baptism.

The middle words of Torah are, "And Moses diligently sought the goat of the sin offering."[26] Paul says that Yeshua *is* the sin offering.[27] Seeking Yeshua is the central goal of Torah. This is one reason Yeshua said that Moses wrote of Him.[28]

When a Gentile woman begged Yeshua for healing, He answered that it wasn't right to take Israel's bread and toss it to the dogs. He just called her a dog, and she agreed! "Truth, Lord: yet the dogs eat of the crumbs which fall from their masters' table."[29] Yeshua granted her request.

Are we ready like the dove, Moses, and the Gentile woman to seek, seek salvation in Yeshua? Can we do it without rejecting Torah or kicking Israel away from the table?

Gentiles portrayed Jesus as a Torah-breaking Christ and Paul as a Torah-breaking apostle. The church tormented Israel and lost its way. But we can return to the church's true foundation: Written and Living Torah. It's time to seek, seek.

With King David let us say, "I delight to do thy will, O my God: yea, thy **Torah** *is* within my heart."[30] To put it another way, *"Torah! Torah! Torah!"*

—Peter Thalhofer, Vashon Island, April 2015/Nisan 5775

Terms

Torah   Torah is the first five books of the Bible: Genesis—בְּרֵאשִׁית *B'reisheet* In the Beginning, Exodus—שְׁמוֹת *Shemot* Names, Leviticus—וַיִּקְרָא *Vayikra* And He Called, Numbers—בְּמִדְבַּר *B'midbar* In the Wilderness, and Deuteronomy—דְּבָרִים *Devarim* Words. The names tell a short story: In the beginning, He called out names into the wilderness, and these are the Words. Usually translated Law, תּוֹרָה *Torah* is from the root יָרָה *yarah* teach, sprinkle like rain, lay a foundation. Yeshua is our Teacher, Living Torah Who, like rain, brings life from heaven to earth, and Who taught us how to live on Written Torah's foundation. Written Torah is our instruction. Living Torah is our example.

Many believers say that they believe Torah. "I love the whole Word of God, including the books of Moses!" But they allow an old flame to compete for attention. Imagine if a bride said to her husband, "Honey, you know I love you, but before we met, my boyfriend and I celebrated our anniversary. So I would like to keep celebrating that date instead of ours. Don't think that I don't love you, it's just easier for me!" The "Bride of Christ" allows unbiblical traditions to replace Torah's calendar, appointed times, and menu. The church convinced believers that Torah is impossible to keep and that Jesus replaced Torah with Grace. It's time to return to the truth.

God's Name LORD in all capitals is an English designation for one of God's Names, יְהוָה *YHVH*. There is much debate over whether or not to try to pronounce this Name in Hebrew. Jews usually substitute *Adonai* Lord or *HaShem* The Name.

Yeshua   The original name of Jesus is יֵשׁוּעַ *Yeshua*, shortened from יְהוֹשׁוּעַ *Yehoshua* Joshua, God is Salvation.[31] In Matthew 1.21 of the KJV 1611 edition, God commanded Joseph, "And she shall bring forth a sonne, and thou shalt call his Name Iesus: for hee shall saue his people from their sinnes." The "J" in Jesus didn't come into popular use until after that first edition, *1,600 years after Yeshua*. Joseph (Yosef) was *commanded* to call his son Yeshua. We can too.

Messiah   Christians accept the death of Jesus Christ on the cross as God's provision for forgiving sin. Receiving this gift of forgiveness by faith, a believer is granted eternal life. Yeshua said in Matthew 5 that He fulfilled Torah. Although most aren't as blunt as Luther, the church believes that by fulfilling Torah, Jesus really abolished it. Experts say that the calendar, appointed times, and menu don't apply now. Even Bible students don't know the Bible's definition of the New Covenant, which includes Torah written in the heart. So the church is comfortable with a Torah-breaking Jesus Christ.

Jews hear from the church that Jesus abolished Torah and, based on Deuteronomy 13, consider Jesus a false prophet. Maimonides is one of the most influential Jewish sages of all time. His twelfth-century *Mishneh Torah* is an authoritative work in Judaism.   He said there,

> Jesus of Nazareth who aspired to be the Mashiach and was executed by the court was also alluded to in Daniel's prophecies, as ibid. 11:14 states: "The vulgar among your people shall exalt themselves in an attempt to fulfill the vision, but they shall stumble." Can there be a greater stumbling block than Christianity? All the prophets spoke of Mashiach as the redeemer of Israel and their savior who would gather their dispersed and strengthen their observance of the mitzvot [Torah commands]. In contrast, Christianity caused the Jews to be slain by the sword, their remnants to be scattered and humbled, the Torah to be altered, and the majority of the world to err and serve a god other than the Lord.[32]

Christians may think that Daniel 11.14 refers to zealots like Judas, who stumbled by trying to push Jesus into declaring himself the King of Israel. But for Jews who know Torah, the church's Jesus Christ *caused the Torah to be altered* and made himself a false prophet. That Torah-breaking Gentile Jesus, however, is not the same as the Bible's Jewish Yeshua, Living Torah Who always upheld Written Torah.

Synagogue   James 2.2 says, "For if a man should come into your meeting..." The Greek word translated meeting is συναγωγή *synagōgē* synagogue.   Translating it simply as meeting is a way to make the church forget that *it used to meet in synagogues—with Jews!*   Accurate translation is kept where it hurts the Jews, however, such as Revelation 2.9, the synagogue of Satan.

Church   Most think ἐκκλησία *ecclesia* called out refers only to the New Covenant church.   It's usually translated church, but ecclesia means any assembly.   To protect the church's image, a rioting ecclesia of Ephesian idolaters is translated assembly, not church, in Acts 19.32, 39, and 41.   In the Septuagint, the Greek translation of Tenach, the Hebrew קָהֵל *qahal* assembly is translated as the Greek ecclesia about eighty times, always referring to Israel.   And ecclesia is the word Stephen used in Acts 7.38 for Moses and Israel in the wilderness.   There was no Gothic building full of Gentiles in the wilderness.   Israel is the Bible's only assembly of God.

Gospel   Hebrews 4.2 says that Israel heard the Gospel in the wilderness.   That's 1,300 years or more before Yeshua.   Galatians 3.8 adds that Abraham had the Gospel centuries before that.   And in Genesis 3.15, God promised that the Seed of woman would defeat the Serpent.   The Gospel is thousands of years older than the Christian church.

Appointed Times   Leviticus 23 describes מוֹעֲדִים *moadim* appointed times.   The church calls these "feasts of the Jews," but they are מוֹעֲדֵי יְהוָה *moadei YHVH* appointed times of the LORD, when God promises to meet His people.   Genesis 1.14 says that the sun and moon are אֹתֹת *otot* signs, signals for these moadim. By abandoning Torah's calendar and adopting the Julian/Gregorian calendar which neglects the moon, the church lost its guide to moadim.   The church doesn't know how Yeshua fulfilled the first four moadim to the day or what to expect when Yeshua returns.   *Trumpets* is the next critical appointed time.   That should sound an alarm!   Chapter 2 explains how Yeshua fulfills Torah's appointed times.

Olive Tree   In Romans 11, Gentile believers in Yeshua are a wild olive shoot *grafted into* the cultivated Olive Tree of Israel.   Gentile believers don't *replace* the Olive Tree. Jeremiah 16.19 says that Gentiles from the ends of the earth will say, "Surely our fathers have inherited lies, vanity, and *things* wherein *there is* no profit."   That verse rings true even now as Gentiles turn from manmade traditions to Torah.

Symbols   In the next chapter, each Thesis shares its page number and is assigned a symbol related to the Lord's Prayer:

Our Father
in Heaven

Your
Name be
sanctified

Your
Kingdom
be blessed

Your will
be done in
heaven and
on earth

Give us
today our
daily bread

Forgive
our debt of
sin as we
forgive
others'

Bring us
not into a
test, but
protect us
from evil

Chapter 1
Torah's Ninety-Five Theses

Think not that I am come to destroy the **Torah**, or the prophets: I am not come to destroy, but to fulfil.

For verily I say unto you, Till heaven and earth pass, one jot or one tittle shall in no wise pass from **Torah**, till all be fulfilled.

Whosoever therefore shall break one of these least commandments, and shall teach men so, he shall be called the least in the kingdom of heaven: but whosoever shall do and teach *them*, the same shall be called great in the kingdom of heaven.

Matthew 5.17-19

This passage shatters all church traditions which insist that Torah has been abolished or that Yeshua changed Torah.
Look up and see heaven. Look down and see earth.
God's eternal Torah is still in force today.
The church aims for the *bottom*
of the Kingdom of Heaven!

Aim for the top.
Keep Torah.

Testimony of the New Covenant: Jeremiah

Behold, the days come, saith the LORD, that I will make a new covenant with the house of Israel, and with the house of Judah:

Not according to the covenant that I made with their fathers in the day *that* I took them by the hand to bring them out of the land of Egypt; which my covenant they brake, although I was an husband unto them, saith the LORD:

But this *shall be* the covenant that I will make with the house of Israel; After those days, saith the LORD, I will put my **Torah** in their inward parts, and write it in their hearts; and will be their God, and they shall be my people.

And they shall teach no more every man his neighbour, and every man his brother, saying, Know the LORD: for they shall all know me, from the least of them unto the greatest of them, saith the LORD:
for I will forgive their iniquity, and I will remember their sin no more.

Jeremiah 31.31-34

The New Covenant is with Israel, not "the church."
The New Covenant is Torah written in the heart.
The New Covenant is forgiveness of sin.

Torah in the heart.

Testimony of the New Covenant: Hebrews

For finding fault with them, he saith, Behold, the days come, saith the Lord, when I will make a new covenant with the house of Israel and with the house of Judah:

Not according to the covenant that I made with their fathers in the day when I took them by the hand to lead them out of the land of Egypt; because they continued not in my covenant, and I regarded them not, saith the Lord.

For this *is* the covenant that I will make with the house of Israel after those days, saith the Lord; I will put my **Torah** into their mind, and write [it] in their hearts: and I will be to them a God, and they shall be to me a people:

And they shall not teach every man his neighbour, and every man his brother, saying, Know the Lord: for all shall know me, from the least to the greatest.

For I will be merciful to their unrighteousness, and their sins and their iniquities will I remember no more.

Hebrews 8.8-12

____

Hebrews quotes Jeremiah for the New Covenant's DNA: Israel, Torah, and forgiveness.

The church rejects 2/3 of the New Covenant.

Testimony of Psalm 1

Blessed *is* the man that walketh not in the counsel of the ungodly, nor standeth in the way of sinners, nor sitteth in the seat of the scornful.

But his delight *is* in the **Torah** of the LORD; and in his **Torah** doth he meditate day and night.

Psalm 1.1-2

———————————

The blessed man delights in Torah and meditates on Torah.

God wants transformation— through Torah.

Testimony of Psalm 19

The **Torah** of the LORD *is* perfect, converting the soul: the testimony of the LORD *is* sure, making wise the simple.

The statutes of the LORD *are* right, rejoicing the heart: the commandment of the LORD *is* pure, enlightening the eyes.

The fear of the LORD *is* clean, enduring for ever: the judgments of the LORD *are* true *and* righteous altogether.

More to be desired *are they* than gold, yea, than much fine gold: sweeter also than honey and the honeycomb.

Moreover by them is thy servant warned: *and* in keeping of them *there is* great reward.

Psalm 19.7-11

Torah is perfect, sure, right, pure, clean, true, and righteous.
Torah is more desirable than gold or honey.
Torah brings warning and reward.

God promises rewards for keeping Torah.
The church promises curses.
Whom should we believe?

A History of Torah Testimony

Testimony of Abraham

Because that Abraham obeyed my voice, and kept my charge, my commandments, my statutes, and my **Torah.**

Genesis 26.5

And the scripture, foreseeing that God would justify the heathen through faith, preached before the gospel unto Abraham, *saying,* In thee shall all nations be blessed.

Galatians 3.8

4,000 years ago...
Abraham kept Torah and Gospel.

Keep Torah and Gospel today.

And it came to pass, that the beggar died, and was carried by the angels into Abraham's bosom: the rich man also died, and was buried;

And in hell he lift up his eyes, being in torments, and seeth Abraham afar off, and Lazarus in his bosom…

Then he said, I pray thee therefore, father, that thou wouldest send him to my father's house:

For I have five brethren; that he may testify unto them, lest they also come into this place of torment.

Abraham saith unto him, They have Moses and the prophets; let them hear them.

And he said, Nay, father Abraham: but if one went unto them from the dead, they will repent.

And he said unto him, If they hear not Moses and the prophets, neither will they be persuaded, though one rose from the dead.

Luke 16.22-23, 27-31

In Yeshua's parable, poor Lazarus and a rich man have died. Tormented, the rich man begs Abraham to warn his family. Perhaps a messenger from the dead will cause repentance. Abraham refuses. Torah and Tenach are witness enough.

Torah leads us to repentance.

Testimony of Moses

And the LORD said unto Moses, Come up to me into the mount, and be there: and I will give thee tables of stone, and a **Torah**, and commandments which I have written; that thou mayest teach them.

Exodus 24.12

And he gave unto Moses, when he had made an end of communing with him upon mount Sinai, two tables of testimony, tables of stone, written with the finger of God.

Exodus 31.18

But if I with the finger of God cast out devils, no doubt the kingdom of God is come upon you.

Luke 11.20

But if I cast out devils by the Spirit of God, then the kingdom of God is come unto you.

Matthew 12.28

God wrote Torah on stone tablets with His finger.
Yeshua equated the finger of God with the Spirit of God.

God's Spirit wrote Torah.
How could Spirit and Torah be at odds now?

And the LORD said unto Moses, I have seen this people, and, behold, it *is* a stiffnecked people:

Now therefore let me alone, that my wrath may wax hot against them, and that I may consume them: and I will make of thee a great nation.

And Moses besought the LORD his God, and said, LORD, why doth thy wrath wax hot against thy people, which thou hast brought forth out of the land of Egypt with great power, and with a mighty hand?

Wherefore should the Egyptians speak, and say, For mischief did he bring them out, to slay them in the mountains, and to consume them from the face of the earth? Turn from thy fierce wrath, and repent of this evil against thy people.

Remember Abraham, Isaac, and Israel, thy servants, to whom thou swarest by thine own self, and saidst unto them, I will multiply your seed as the stars of heaven, and all this land that I have spoken of will I give unto your seed, and they shall inherit *it* for ever.

And the LORD repented of the evil which he thought to do unto his people.

Exodus 32.9-14

Israel worshipped the Golden Calf as Moses received Torah.
In His anger, God wanted to destroy Israel.
Moses argued from Torah.
God repented.

Torah is the basis for God's forgiveness.

And the LORD descended in the cloud, and stood with him there, and proclaimed the name of the LORD.

And the LORD passed by before him, and proclaimed, The LORD, The LORD God, merciful and gracious, longsuffering, and abundant in goodness and truth,

Keeping mercy for thousands, forgiving iniquity and transgression and sin, and that will by no means clear *the guilty*; visiting the iniquity of the fathers upon the children, and upon the children's children, unto the third and to the fourth *generation*.

And Moses made haste, and bowed his head toward the earth, and worshipped.

Exodus 34.5-8

After the Golden Calf, Israel needed God's presence.
Moses found Grace in God's sight.
God revealed His glory:

יְהֹוָה, Grace, mercy, patience, goodness, truth, and justice.
The same God yesterday and today.

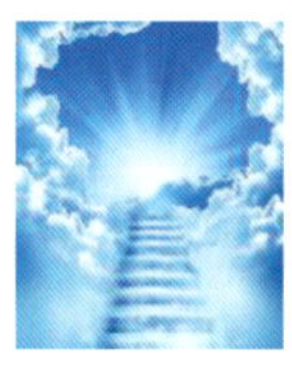

Torah is God's Grace revealed.

Ye shall have one **Torah** for him that sinneth through ignorance, *both for* him that is born among the children of Israel, and for the stranger that sojourneth among them.

Numbers 15.29

Speak unto the children of Israel, and bid them that they make them fringes in the borders of their garments throughout their generations, and that they put upon the fringe of the borders a ribband of blue:

And it shall be unto you for a fringe, that ye may look upon it, and remember all the commandments of the LORD, and do them; and that ye seek not after your own heart and your own eyes, after which ye use to go a whoring:

That ye may remember, and do all my commandments, and be holy unto your God.

Numbers 15.38-40

———————————

One Torah for Israel and Gentiles.
Wear *tzitzit* to do Torah and to be holy.
Tzitzit are white and blue cords attached to
corners of a garment which flutter in the wind,
so these tzitzit came to earn the nickname "wings."
The sick woman in Matthew 9.20 touched Yeshua's
κράσπεδον *kraspedon* fringe/tzitzit and received healing.
She trusted Malachi 4.2a, "But unto you that fear my name
shall the Sun of righteousness arise with healing in his wings."

Tzitzit: God's ID badge.

Hear, O Israel: The LORD our God *is* one LORD:

And thou shalt love the LORD thy God with all thine heart, and with all thy soul, and with all thy might.

And these words, which I command thee this day, shall be in thine heart:

And thou shalt teach them diligently unto thy children, and shalt talk of them when thou sittest in thine house, and when thou walkest by the way, and when thou liest down, and when thou risest up.

And thou shalt bind them for a sign upon thine hand, and they shall be as frontlets between thine eyes.

And thou shalt write them upon the posts of thy house, and on thy gates.

Deuteronomy 6.4-9

Love God.
Write Torah in the heart.
Teach Torah diligently to children.
Bind Torah on hands, foreheads, doorposts, and gates.

Tefillin, boxes for arms and foreheads, contain Torah verses.
Mezuzot, for doorposts and gates, also contain verses.
Yeshua would have used both.
Do we?

Tefillin and mezuzot: God's ID badges.

And it shall be, when he sitteth upon the throne of his kingdom, that he shall write him a copy of this **Torah** in a book out of *that which is* before the priests the Levites:

And it shall be with him, and he shall read therein all the days of his life: that he may learn to fear the LORD his God, to keep all the words of this **Torah** and these statutes, to do them:

That his heart be not lifted up above his brethren, and that he turn not aside from the commandment, *to* the right hand, or *to* the left: to the end that he may prolong *his* days in his kingdom, he, and his children, in the midst of Israel.

Deuteronomy 17.18-20

———————————————

The king is to write his own copy of Torah and do it.

Kings are under Torah's authority.

The secret *things belong* unto the Lord our God: but those *things which are* revealed *belong* unto us and to our children for ever, that *we* may do all the words of this **Torah**.

Deuteronomy 29.29

––––––––––––––––––––––

עוֹלָם *olam* is translated for ever.

Olam is used in Genesis 9.16 when God
promised never again to destroy with a flood.
Olam is used in Exodus 21.2-6 to describe the
process for a man to choose to be a slave forever,
and Exodus 27.20-21 to describe the lamp which is
to burn forever in the Tabernacle or the Temple.
Yet the slave died and the lamp was destroyed.
So how can we know that Torah is forever?

God ended both slave and Temple.
God never ended the rainbow.
God never ended Torah.

Torah forever.

And the LORD thy God will make thee plenteous in every work of thine hand, in the fruit of thy body, and in the fruit of thy cattle, and in the fruit of thy land, for good: for the LORD will again rejoice over thee for good, as he rejoiced over thy fathers:

If thou shalt hearken unto the voice of the LORD thy God, to keep his commandments and his statutes which are written in this book of the **Torah**, *and* if thou turn unto the LORD thy God with all thine heart, and with all thy soul.

For this commandment which I command thee this day, it *is* not hidden from thee, neither *is* it far off.

It *is* not in heaven, that thou shouldest say, Who shall go up for us to heaven, and bring it unto us, that we may hear it, and do it?

Neither *is* it beyond the sea, that thou shouldest say, Who shall go over the sea for us, and bring it unto us, that we may hear it, and do it?

But the word *is* very nigh unto thee, in thy mouth, and in thy heart, that thou mayest do it.

Deuteronomy 30.9-14

Keeping Torah brings blessing.
The church says that it's impossible.
But Luke 1.6 says of Zacharias and Elisabeth,
 "And they were both righteous before God, walking in
all the commandments and ordinances of the Lord blameless."

Just do it.

And Moses wrote this **Torah**, and delivered it unto the priests the sons of Levi, which bare the ark of the covenant of the LORD, and unto all the elders of Israel.

And Moses commanded them, saying, At the end of *every* seven years, in the solemnity of the year of release, in the feast of tabernacles,

When all Israel is come to appear before the LORD thy God in the place which he shall choose, thou shalt read this **Torah** before all Israel in their hearing.

Gather the people together, men, and women, and children, and thy stranger that *is* within thy gates, that they may hear, and that they may learn, and fear the LORD your God, and observe to do all the words of this **Torah:**

And *that* their children, which have not known *any thing*, may hear, and learn to fear the LORD your God, as long as ye live in the land whither ye go over Jordan to possess it.

Deuteronomy 31.9-13

Just before he died, Moses set the Feast of Tabernacles as the occasion to read Torah. All Israel *and the Gentiles* are to hear and learn to fear God, and to do Torah.

After Messiah returns to the Mt. of Olives, Zechariah 14.4, verses 16-19 describe how nations that fought against Jerusalem will go up to celebrate Tabernacles and learn Torah, or they will get plague and drought.

Torah and Tabernacles were good.
They will be good in the last days.
How could they be bad now?

Testimony of Joshua

This book of the **Torah** shall not depart out of thy mouth; but thou shalt meditate therein day and night, that thou mayest observe to do according to all that is written therein: for then thou shalt make thy way prosperous, and then thou shalt have good success.

Have not I commanded thee? Be strong and of a good courage; be not afraid, neither be thou dismayed: for the LORD thy God *is* with thee whithersoever thou goest.

Joshua 1.8-9

———————————

God prepared Joshua to conquer Canaan by keeping Torah.
Not a priest, Joshua couldn't do all of Torah.
But he did everything he could.

Conquer with Torah.

I delight to do thy will, O my God:
yea, thy **Torah** *is* within my heart.

Psalm 40.8

———————————————

500 years before Jeremiah wrote about the New Covenant...
1,000 years before Yeshua founded the New Covenant...
3,000 years before we forgot the New Covenant...
King David understood the New Covenant.

Torah in the heart.

Now the days of David drew nigh that he should die; and he charged Solomon his son, saying,

I go the way of all the earth: be thou strong therefore, and shew thyself a man;

And keep the charge of the LORD thy God, to walk in his ways, to keep his statutes, and his commandments, and his judgments, and his testimonies, as it is written in the **Torah** of Moses, that thou mayest prosper in all that thou doest, and whithersoever thou turnest thyself:

1 Kings 2.1-3

King David knew that obedience results in a prosperous life. He hoped that his son Solomon would follow Torah.

Moses warned in Deuteronomy 17.14-17 that any future king of Israel should not accumulate horses, wives, or wealth. Solomon broke all those commands and more.

1 Kings 11 says that Solomon built altars to Chemosh and Molech to please his foreign wives. Some of Solomon's children likely passed through the fire for those idols. God promised to tear apart Solomon's Kingdom.

During the reign of Solomon's son, God divided Israel. Two southern tribes became the Kingdom of Judah. Ten northern tribes became the Kingdom of Israel.

Sometimes Solomon kept Torah; sometimes he didn't. Solomon's divided heart led to a divided Kingdom.

Be wiser than Solomon.
Stick with Torah.

Testimony of Hosea

My people are destroyed for lack of knowledge: because thou
hast rejected knowledge, I will also reject thee, that thou shalt
be no priest to me: seeing thou hast forgotten the **Torah** of thy
God, I will also forget thy children.

Hosea 4.6

God warned Israel through Hosea not to forget the Torah.
God told Hosea to marry a prostitute, so Hosea would
know how God felt being married to unfaithful Israel.
Israel ignored God's warnings through Hosea.
God sent Assyria against Israel in 722 BC.

We usually don't hear all of Hosea 4.6.
What lack brought destruction?
Lack of knowledge of Torah.
The church lacks Torah.

Forgetting Torah leads to destruction.

Set the trumpet to thy mouth. *He shall come* as an eagle against the house of the LORD, because they have transgressed my covenant, and trespassed against my **Torah**.

Israel shall cry unto me, My God, we know thee.*

Israel hath cast off *the thing that is* good: the enemy shall pursue him…

I have written to him the great things of my **Torah**, *but* they were counted as a strange thing.

Hosea 8.1-3, 12

Israel didn't listen to God's warnings and broke Torah.
Israel rejected good. The enemy pursued him.
Israel cried to God, but it was too late.

Israel counted Torah as strange.
The church counts Torah as strange.

Counting Torah as strange angers God.

* Thesis 74

Testimony of the Author of II Kings

Yet the LORD testified against Israel, and against Judah, by all the prophets, *and by* all the seers, saying, Turn ye from your evil ways, and keep my commandments *and* my statutes, according to all the **Torah** which I commanded your fathers, and which I sent to you by my servants the prophets.

Notwithstanding they would not hear, but hardened their necks, like to the neck of their fathers, that did not believe in the LORD their God.

And they rejected his statutes, and his covenant that he made with their fathers, and his testimonies which he testified against them; and they followed vanity, and became vain, and went after the heathen that *were* round about them, *concerning* whom the LORD had charged them, that they should not do like them.

And they left all the commandments of the LORD their God, and made them molten images, *even* two calves, and made a grove, and worshipped all the host of heaven, and served Baal.

And they caused their sons and their daughters to pass through the fire, and used divination and enchantments, and sold themselves to do evil in the sight of the LORD, to provoke him to anger.

Therefore the LORD was very angry with Israel, and removed them out of his sight: there was none left but the tribe of Judah only.

2 Kings 17.13-18

 Rejecting Torah leads to destruction.

Testimony of Amos

Thus saith the LORD; For three transgressions of Judah, and for four, I will not turn away *the punishment* thereof; because they have despised the **Torah** of the LORD, and have not kept his commandments, and their lies caused them to err, after the which their fathers have walked:

But I will send a fire upon Judah, and it shall devour the palaces of Jerusalem.

Amos 2.4-5

Amos warned Judah of punishment for despising Torah. Babylon burned Jerusalem in 586 BC.

Despising Torah brings fire.

Testimony of Micah

But in the last days it shall come to pass, *that* the mountain of the house of the LORD shall be established in the top of the mountains, and it shall be exalted above the hills; and people shall flow unto it.

And many nations shall come, and say, Come, and let us go up to the mountain of the LORD, and to the house of the God of Jacob; and he will teach us of his ways, and we will walk in his paths: for the **Torah** shall go forth of Zion, and the word of the LORD from Jerusalem.

Micah 4.1-2

———————————————

In the last days, nations will study Torah in Jerusalem.

Torah was good.
Torah will be good in the last days.
How could Torah possibly be bad now?

Testimony of Isaiah

And it shall come to pass in the last days, *that* the mountain of the LORD'S house shall be established in the top of the mountains, and shall be exalted above the hills; and all nations shall flow unto it.

And many people shall go and say, Come ye, and let us go up to the mountain of the LORD, to the house of the God of Jacob; and he will teach us of his ways, and we will walk in his paths: for out of Zion shall go forth the **Torah**, and the word of the LORD from Jerusalem.

Isaiah 2.2-3

Isaiah repeated Micah's message.

Hebrew is the language of Israel and Torah. Study Torah in Hebrew in Jerusalem.

To the **Torah** and to the testimony: if they speak not according to this word, *it is* because *there is* no light in them.

Isaiah 8.20

———————————

Speak according to Torah.

O Assyrian, the rod of mine anger, and the staff in their hand is mine indignation.

I will send him against an hypocritical nation, and against the people of my wrath will I give him a charge, to take the spoil, and to take the prey, and to tread them down like the mire of the streets.

Isaiah 10.5-6

____

The Assyrians were feared for their savage cruelty.
They cut off noses, ears, limbs, and gouged eyes.
They flayed victims' skin and left them to die.
They impaled victims and cut off heads.
God sent *terrorists* against Israel—
for rejecting his Torah!

Torah hypocrisy brings terror.

Behold my servant, whom I uphold; mine elect, *in whom* my soul delighteth; I have put my spirit upon him: he shall bring forth judgment to the Gentiles.

He shall not cry, nor lift up, nor cause his voice to be heard in the street.

A bruised reed shall he not break, and the smoking flax shall he not quench: he shall bring forth judgment unto truth.

He shall not fail nor be discouraged, till he have set judgment in the earth: and the isles shall wait for his **Torah**.

Isaiah 42.1-4

Behold my servant, whom I have chosen; my beloved, in whom my soul is well pleased: I will put my spirit upon him, and he shall shew judgment to the Gentiles.

He shall not strive, nor cry; neither shall any man hear his voice in the streets.

A bruised reed shall he not break, and smoking flax shall he not quench, till he send forth judgment unto victory.

And in his name shall the Gentiles trust.

Matthew 12.18-21

Matthew quoted Isaiah, referring to Yeshua.
Note the change to the last verse.

Yeshua is Torah.

Testimony of King Josiah

And it came to pass, when the king had heard the words of the book of the **Torah**, that he rent his clothes.

And the king commanded Hilkiah the priest, and Ahikam the son of Shaphan, and Achbor the son of Michaiah, and Shaphan the scribe, and Asahiah a servant of the king's, saying,

Go ye, enquire of the LORD for me, and for the people, and for all Judah, concerning the words of this book that is found: for great *is* the wrath of the LORD that is kindled against us, because our fathers have not hearkened unto the words of this book, to do according unto all that which is written concerning us.

2 Kings 22.11-13

In the Kingdom of Judah before its destruction,
King Josiah took the throne at the age of eight.
At twenty-six, he renovated the Temple.
Workers discovered a Torah scroll
among the idols in the Temple.

Josiah grieved and repented at how Judah turned from God.
Because of Josiah's humility, God delayed Judah's fate.
But kings after Josiah ignored Torah.
Destruction followed.

Josiah earned a stay of execution
by seeking Torah.

Testimony of Zephaniah

Woe to her that is filthy and polluted, to the oppressing city!

She obeyed not the voice; she received not correction; she trusted not in the LORD; she drew not near to her God.

Her princes within her *are* roaring lions; her judges *are* evening wolves; they gnaw not the bones till the morrow.

Her prophets *are* light *and* treacherous persons: her priests have polluted the sanctuary, they have done violence to the **Torah.**

Zephaniah 3.1-4

Zephaniah was one of Judah's last prophets before war. One reason why Jerusalem deserved judgment: Prophets and priests violated Torah.

Violating Torah brings war.

Testimony of Jeremiah

Thus saith the LORD, What iniquity have your fathers found in me, that they are gone far from me, and have walked after vanity, and are become vain?

Neither said they, Where is the LORD that brought us up out of the land of Egypt, that led us through the wilderness, through a land of deserts and of pits, through a land of drought, and of the shadow of death, through a land that no man passed through, and where no man dwelt?

And I brought you into a plentiful country, to eat the fruit thereof and the goodness thereof; but when ye entered, ye defiled my land, and made mine heritage an abomination.

The priests said not, Where *is* the LORD? and they that handle the **Torah** knew me not: the pastors also transgressed against me, and the prophets prophesied by Baal, and walked after *things that* do not profit.

Wherefore I will yet plead with you, saith the LORD, and with your children's children will I plead.

Jeremiah 2.5-9

Jeremiah prophesied before, during, and after Judah's exile. Priests, pastors, and prophets ignored God and Torah. God רִיב *reev* pleads, strives, quarrels with them.

God quarrels with ministers who ignore Torah.

For thus saith the LORD of hosts, the God of Israel; Behold, I will cause to cease out of this place in your eyes, and in your days, the voice of mirth, and the voice of gladness, the voice of the bridegroom, and the voice of the bride.

And it shall come to pass, when thou shalt shew this people all these words, and they shall say unto thee, Wherefore hath the LORD pronounced all this great evil against us? or what *is* our iniquity? or what *is* our sin that we have committed against the LORD our God?

Then shalt thou say unto them, Because your fathers have forsaken me, saith the LORD, and have walked after other gods, and have served them, and have worshipped them, and have forsaken me, and have not kept my **Torah**;

And ye have done worse than your fathers; for, behold, ye walk every one after the imagination of his evil heart, that they may not hearken unto me:

Therefore will I cast you out of this land into a land that ye know not, *neither* ye nor your fathers; and there shall ye serve other gods day and night; where I will not shew you favour.

Jeremiah 16.9-13

The fathers broke Torah; the children did worse.
Everyone walked after his or her own heart.

Judah wouldn't give up their idols.
God exiled Judah to serve idols.

Forsaking Torah causes exile.

Testimony of Daniel

To the Lord our God belong mercies and forgivenesses, though we have rebelled against him;

Neither have we obeyed the voice of the LORD our God, to walk in his **Torah**, which he set before us by his servants the prophets.

Yea, all Israel have transgressed thy **Torah**, even by departing, that they might not obey thy voice; therefore the curse is poured upon us, and the oath that *is* written in the **Torah** of Moses the servant of God, because we have sinned against him.

And he hath confirmed his words, which he spake against us, and against our judges that judged us, by bringing upon us a great evil: for under the whole heaven hath not been done as hath been done upon Jerusalem.

As *it is* written in the **Torah** of Moses, all this evil is come upon us: yet made we not our prayer before the LORD our God, that we might turn from our iniquities, and understand thy truth.

Daniel 9.9-13

Babylon took young Daniel captive and prized his wisdom.
Risking his life, Daniel kept Torah even in Babylon.
In Daniel's old age, Persia conquered Babylon.
Seventy years of exile would soon be completed.
In verse 9.11, Daniel knew that Israel's transgressing of
Torah caused God to pour out the אָלָה *alah* curse on Israel.

Transgressing Torah brings the curse.

Testimony of Ezekiel

Son of man, say unto her, Thou *art* the land that is not cleansed, nor rained upon in the day of indignation.

There is a conspiracy of her prophets in the midst thereof, like a roaring lion ravening the prey; they have devoured souls; they have taken the treasure and precious things; they have made her many widows in the midst thereof.

Her priests have violated my **Torah**, and have profaned mine holy things: they have put no difference between the holy and profane, neither have they shewed *difference* between the unclean and the clean, and have hid their eyes from my sabbaths, and I am profaned among them.

Ezekiel 22.24-26

Like Daniel, Ezekiel lived during the Babylonian exile.
Like Daniel, Ezekiel saw God's judgment for breaking Torah.

God exiled His people from Israel and burned His Temple—because prophets and priests violated Torah and Sabbath.

When Torah is violated,
God is profaned.

And they shall teach my people *the difference* between the holy and profane, and cause them to discern between the unclean and the clean.

And in controversy they shall stand in judgment; *and* they shall judge it according to my judgments: and they shall keep my **Torah** and my statutes in all mine assemblies; and they shall hallow my sabbaths.

Ezekiel 44.23-24

Ezekiel prophesied a return from exile and a new Temple.
Both these happened before Yeshua's ministry.
But we are seeing a greater return today.
And a greater Temple is imminent.

In the coming Temple, priests honor Torah and Sabbath.
Priests keep the appointed times.
They judge by Torah.

Torah, Sabbath, and appointed times were good and will be good again. How could they be bad now?

Testimony of Ezra

For Ezra had prepared his heart to seek the **Torah** of the LORD, and to do *it*, and to teach in Israel statutes and judgments.

Ezra 7.10

———————————

Ezra prepared his heart to seek Torah.
So he was commissioned to restore worship in Israel.
In the fifth century BC, the king of Persia's letter said in part,

"And I, *even* I Artaxerxes the king, do make a decree to all the treasurers which *are* beyond the river, that whatsoever Ezra the priest, the scribe of the **Torah** of the God of heaven, shall require of you, it be done speedily."

Ezra's Great Assembly finalized Tenach's
canon and Torah portions, standardized the calendar,
and wrote prayers with Nehemiah, Mordechai, Zerubbabel,
Haggai, Zechariah, Malachi, and others, 120 ministers in all.

Yeshua followed the work of the Great Assembly.
He prayed their prayers and followed their Torah portions.

Prepare for your mission.
Study Torah.

Testimony of Nehemiah

And Ezra opened the book in the sight of all the people; (for he was above all the people;) and when he opened it, all the people stood up:

And Ezra blessed the LORD, the great God. And all the people answered, Amen, Amen, with lifting up their hands: and they bowed their heads, and worshipped the LORD with *their* faces to the ground.

Also Jeshua, and Bani, and Sherebiah, Jamin, Akkub, Shabbethai, Hodijah, Maaseiah, Kelita, Azariah, Jozabad, Hanan, Pelaiah, and the Levites, caused the people to understand the **Torah**: and the people *stood* in their place.

So they read in the book in the **Torah** of God distinctly, and gave the sense, and caused *them* to understand the reading.

And Nehemiah, which *is* the Tirshatha, and Ezra the priest the scribe, and the Levites that taught the people, said unto all the people, This day *is* holy unto the LORD your God; mourn not, nor weep. For all the people wept, when they heard the words of the **Torah**.

Nehemiah 8.5-9

Ezra and Nehemiah taught Torah at Tabernacles.
This appointed time had been overlooked since Joshua.
The people wept at Torah like Josiah; then they celebrated.

Torah's appointed times return us to God.

Testimony of Zechariah

Thus speaketh the LORD of hosts, saying, Execute true judgment, and shew mercy and compassions every man to his brother:

And oppress not the widow, nor the fatherless, the stranger, nor the poor; and let none of you imagine evil against his brother in your heart.

But they refused to hearken, and pulled away the shoulder, and stopped their ears, that they should not [שָׁמַע *shama*] hear.

Yea, they made their hearts *as* an adamant stone, lest they should [shama] the **Torah**, and the words which the LORD of hosts hath sent in his spirit by the former prophets: therefore came a great wrath from the LORD of hosts.

Therefore it is come to pass, *that* as he cried, and they would not [shama]; so they cried, and I would not [shama], saith the LORD of hosts:

But I scattered them with a whirlwind among all the nations whom they knew not. Thus the land was desolate after them, that no man passed through nor returned: for they laid the pleasant land desolate.

Zechariah 7.9-14

Zechariah reminded Israel why they were exiled:
They refused to שָׁמַע *shama* hear, obey Torah.

When we refuse to hear Torah,
God refuses to hear us.

Testimony of Malachi

And ye shall know that I have sent this commandment unto you, that my covenant might be with Levi, saith the LORD of hosts.

My covenant was with him of life and peace; and I gave them to him *for* the fear wherewith he feared me, and was afraid before my name.

The **Torah** of truth was in his mouth, and iniquity was not found in his lips: he walked with me in peace and equity, and did turn many away from iniquity.

For the priest's lips should keep knowledge, and they should seek the **Torah** at his mouth: for he *is* the messenger of the LORD of hosts.

But ye are departed out of the way; ye have caused many to stumble at the **Torah**; ye have corrupted the covenant of Levi, saith the LORD of hosts.

Therefore have I also made you contemptible and base before all the people, according as ye have not kept my ways, but have been partial in the **Torah**.

Malachi 2.4-9

Levites avenged Torah after the sin of the Golden Calf. They killed 3,000 Israelites for worshipping the idol. But later priests caused stumbling at Torah.

When priests dishonor Torah, God dishonors the priests.

For, behold, the day cometh, that shall burn as an oven; and all the proud, yea, and all that do wickedly, shall be stubble: and the day that cometh shall burn them up, saith the LORD of hosts, that it shall leave them neither root nor branch.

But unto you that fear my name shall the Sun of righteousness arise with healing in his wings; and ye shall go forth, and grow up as calves of the stall.

And ye shall tread down the wicked; for they shall be ashes under the soles of your feet in the day that I shall do *this*, saith the LORD of hosts.

Remember ye the **Torah** of Moses my servant, which I commanded unto him in Horeb for all Israel, *with* the statutes and judgments.

Behold, I will send you Elijah the prophet before the coming of the great and dreadful day of the LORD:

And he shall turn the heart of the fathers to the children, and the heart of the children to their fathers, lest I come and smite the earth.

Malachi 4

Malachi is Tenach's last prophet, 400 years before Yeshua.
The woman in Matthew 9 believed Malachi (Thesis 11).
The disciples in Matthew 16 and 17 understood.
Yeshua said that Elijah was John the Baptist.
Malachi said to keep remembering Torah.

Messiah and Elijah have come.
Remember Torah.

Testimony of Psalm 119

Blessed *are* the undefiled in the way, who walk in the **Torah** of the LORD.

Psalm 119.1

No psalm is so powerful an advocate for Torah as Psalm 119. As you consider these verses from Psalm 119, ask yourself, "If I believe that the Bible is the Word of God, how could Torah not be for today?"

Walk in Torah.
Be blessed.

Open thou mine eyes, that I may behold
wondrous things out of thy Torah.

Psalm 119.18

Remove from me the way of lying: and grant me thy **Torah** graciously.

Psalm 119.29

 Torah is a gift of Grace.

Give me understanding, and I shall keep thy **Torah**; yea, I shall observe it with *my* whole heart.

Psalm 119.34

 *If* God gives understanding, we desire Torah.

So shall I keep thy **Torah** continually for ever and ever.

And I will walk at liberty: for I seek thy precepts.

Psalm 119.44-45

Liberty is רָחָב *rachav*.
רָחָב is the root for רְחֹב *rechov* street.
When we follow traffic laws, we drive freely.
Breaking traffic laws leads to painful consequences.

Torah has instructions, warnings, rules, and consequences.
When we follow Torah, we walk in liberty.
Breaking Torah brings suffering.

Torah is liberty.

Horror hath taken hold upon me because of the wicked that forsake thy **Torah**.

Psalm 119.53

———————————————

The wicked forsake Torah.
The church forsakes Torah.

Stop being wicked.
Keep Torah.

I have remembered thy name, O LORD, in the night, and have kept thy **Torah**.

Psalm 119.55

The blessed man meditates on Torah day and night.
Jacob wrestled all night, and was blessed.
God struck the firstborn of Egypt at midnight.
God told Joshua to meditate on Torah also at night.
Gideon attacked in the middle watch of the night.
Samson waited until midnight to break out of Gaza.
Ruth startled Boaz about midnight.
A woman stole another's infant son about midnight.
Nehemiah prayed day and night for Israel.
Wall builders kept watch also at night.
Joseph's family fled from Herod in the night.
Shepherds kept watch at night and saw baby Yeshua.
Anna prayed also at night and recognized Messiah.
Evil men love darkness.
Yeshua prayed all night before choosing the apostles.
Yeshua walked on water during the fourth watch.
The disciples slept at night; Yeshua prayed.
Yeshua's captors used their "power of darkness."
God freed Paul and Silas from jail at midnight.
Paul was shipwrecked at midnight; all were saved.
God will avenge His elect, who cry out also at night.
The bridegroom comes suddenly at midnight.
The Day of the Lord is like a thief in the night.
The four living creatures praise God also at night.[1]

 Remember יְהֹוָה at night.
And keep Torah.

The bands of the wicked have robbed me: *but* I have not forgotten thy **Torah**.

Psalm 119.61

David, likely author of this psalm, could have been bitter.
He wearied for crying and people hated him for no reason.
He was a stranger to his brothers and Saul tried to kill him.
He got vinegar for his thirst and was the song of drunkards.
David cried out for justice. But he never grew bitter at God.

Torah frees us from bitterness.

The **Torah** of thy mouth *is* better unto me than thousands of gold and silver.

Psalm 119.72

———————————————

We spend youth and health to gain wealth.
Then we spend wealth to regain youth and health.

Torah is better than wealth.

Let thy tender mercies come unto me, that I may live: for thy **Torah** *is* my delight.

Psalm 119.77

 Torah is delight.

Unless thy **Torah** *had been* my delights, I should then have perished in mine affliction.

Psalm 119.92

———————————

God rescued those who delighted in Torah: Abraham, Moses, Joshua, Gideon, Ruth, David, Elijah, Daniel, Esther, and many more.

Delight in Torah.
Survive.

MEM. O how love I thy **Torah**! it *is* my meditation all the day.

Psalm 119.97

שִׂיחָה *see-cha* is the word for meditation, prayer, musing. When we are *a-mused*, the opposite of meditation, we waste precious time on silliness.

Don't waste time.
Muse on Torah.

My soul *is* continually in my hand: yet do I not forget thy
Torah.

Psalm 119.109

Our choices affect our lives.

Keep Torah.
Live.

SAMECH. I hate *vain* thoughts: but thy **Torah** do I love.

Psalm 119.113

And Jesus said unto him, No man, having put his hand to the plough, and looking back, is fit for the kingdom of God.

Luke 9.62

Vain thoughts are סְעִפִּים *say-ah-feem*, used once in the Bible. The root is *סֵעֵף *say-afe* ambivalent, divided, half-hearted.

David's whole heart for God and Torah built the Kingdom. Solomon's divided heart divided the Kingdom.

Written and Living Torah
demand a whole heart.

*In Hebrew's picture language, ס stands for סָמַךְ *samach* support, ע is עַיִן *ayin* eye, and פ is פֶּה *peh* mouth. These three letters are consecutive in the Hebrew alphabet, פ-ע-ס. In tradition, the two uprights of ע are a right and left eye. The right eye (on our left) is the evil eye, stinginess, since it looks toward the mouth and satisfying desire. The left eye is the good eye, generosity, looking to support another. If our eyes look toward different goals, we have a divided heart.

It is time for *thee*, LORD, to work: *for* they have made void thy
Torah.

Psalm 119.126

Void is פָּרַר *parar* break, split, divide.
They have broken Torah, and the psalmist is angry.

Don't be one the psalmist prayed against!

Rivers of waters run down mine eyes, because they keep not thy **Torah**.

Psalm 119.136

The psalmist cries: people don't שָׁמַר *shamar* keep Torah. Shamar also means guard, protect, watch, observe.

There is no priesthood or Temple now.
We cannot do many commands.
But we can still guard them.

Watchmen cry when Torah isn't guarded.

Thy righteousness *is* an everlasting righteousness, and thy
Torah *is* the truth.

Psalm 119.142

"I am the way, the truth, and the life: no man cometh unto the
Father, but by me."

John 14.6

Torah = Truth = Yeshua.

RESH. Consider mine affliction, and deliver me: for I do not forget thy **Torah**.

Psalm 119.153

Now therefore, if ye will obey my voice indeed, and keep my covenant, then ye shall be a peculiar treasure unto me above all people: for all the earth *is* mine:

Exodus 19.5

———————————————

Torah is like an ancient Suzerain Treaty:

- The superior kingdom demands allegiance and obedience.
    Exodus 19 is the prelude to the covenant.
    Exodus 20 establishes the covenant.

- Each kingdom keeps a copy of the covenant in its temple.
    A copy of Torah was kept in Israel's Tabernacle.
    Heaven has a Tabernacle, Hebrews 9.1-14.
    A copy is kept there, Revelation 11.19.

- Obedience earns blessings; disobedience earns curses.
    Deuteronomy lists the blessings and curses.

Yeshua told us to pray for God's Kingdom, Matthew 6.9-13.
In Revelation, God's Kingdom is fully realized on earth.

The psalmist expects God's help because He keeps covenant.

Torah keepers expect rescue.

I hate and abhor lying: *but* thy **Torah** do I love.

Psalm 119.163

The psalmist keeps the Ninth Commandment, Exodus 20.16,
"Thou shalt not bear false witness against thy neighbour."
Then he goes further: he hates and abhors lying.

An honest person is a threat to every liar.
He's not worried—God has his back.

Torah lovers hate lies.

Great peace have they which love thy **Torah**: and nothing shall offend them.

Psalm 119.165

Wherefore also it is contained in the scripture, Behold, I lay in Sion a chief corner stone, elect, precious: and he that believeth on him shall not be confounded.

Unto you therefore which believe *he is* precious: but unto them which be disobedient, the stone which the builders disallowed, the same is made the head of the corner,

And a stone of stumbling, and a rock of offence, *even to them* which stumble at the word, being disobedient: whereunto also they were appointed,"

1 Peter 2.6-8

―――――――――――

מִכְשׁוֹל *mich-showl* offend, stumbling block.
Peter says that the stumbling block is Yeshua,
quoting Isaiah 28.16, Psalm 118.22, Isaiah 8.14.
The disobedient stumble on Yeshua and reject Him.

Torah lovers don't stumble.

I have longed for thy salvation, O LORD; and thy **Torah** *is* my delight.

Psalm 119.174

———————————————

Psalm 119's last Torah includes יְשׁוּעָה *yeshua*
salvation, deliverance, and source of יְשׁוּעַ Yeshua.

Torah is the way to walk, it is wonderful, a gift of Grace, understanding, liberty, better than gold or silver, a delight, safety, meditation, the desire of the wholehearted, and truth.

Watchmen are horrified and cry when Torah is forsaken. They remember, won't forget or stumble, and love Torah. They want God to work because of those who break Torah.

Torah keepers expect God to rescue them.

Long for Yeshua.
Delight in Torah.

More Testimonies of Psalms

[Maschil of Asaph.] Give ear, O my people, *to* my **Torah**: incline your ears to the words of my mouth.

I will open my mouth in a parable: I will utter dark sayings of old:

Which we have heard and known, and our fathers have told us.

We will not hide *them* from their children, shewing to the generation to come the praises of the LORD, and his strength, and his wonderful works that he hath done.

For he established a testimony in Jacob, and appointed a **Torah** in Israel, which he commanded our fathers, that they should make them known to their children:

That the generation to come might know *them, even* the children *which* should be born; *who* should arise and declare *them* to their children:

That they might set their hope in God, and not forget the works of God, but keep his commandments:

Psalm 78.1-7

"Generation to come" is דּוֹר אַחֲרוֹן *dowr a'cha'ron.*
Last generation. Terminal generation.
Our generation.

Teach Torah to children.
Now.

If his children forsake my **Torah**, and walk not in my judgments;

If they break my statutes, and keep not my commandments;

Then will I visit their transgression with the rod, and their iniquity with stripes.

Nevertheless my lovingkindness will I not utterly take from him, nor suffer my faithfulness to fail.

My covenant will I not break, nor alter the thing that is gone out of my lips.

Once have I sworn by my holiness that I will not lie unto David.

His seed shall endure for ever, and his throne as the sun before me.

It shall be established for ever as the moon, and *as* a faithful witness in heaven. Selah.

Psalm 89.30-37

God made promises to David, the author of this psalm. David's sons broke Torah, but God kept His promises.

David knew God's promises were really for Messiah. Peter explained David's reasoning in Acts 2.29-36.

God punishes Torah breaking. And still keeps His promises.

Blessed *is* the man whom thou chastenest, O LORD, and teachest him out of thy **Torah**;

That thou mayest give him rest from the days of adversity, until the pit be digged for the wicked.

Psalm 94.12-13

For whom the Lord loveth he chasteneth, and scourgeth every son whom he receiveth.

If ye endure chastening, God dealeth with you as with sons; for what son is he whom the father chasteneth not?

But if ye be without chastisement, whereof all are partakers, then are ye bastards, and not sons.

Furthermore we have had fathers of our flesh which corrected *us*, and we gave *them* reverence: shall we not much rather be in subjection unto the Father of spirits, and live?

Hebrews 12.6-9

יָסַר *yasar* chasten means to correct by punishment,
to inflict pain for the purpose of reclaiming,
to chasten a son with a rod.

God inflicts pain on blessed men.
Without chastening, we're bastards.
After chastening, God teaches by Torah.
Many run from both chastening and Torah.

If we get trapped,
God chastens and teaches from Torah.

For he remembered his holy promise, *and* Abraham his servant.

And he brought forth his people with joy, *and* his chosen with gladness:

And gave them the lands of the heathen: and they inherited the labour of the people;

That they might observe his statutes, and keep his **Torah**. Praise ye the LORD.

Psalm 105.42-45

God blesses His people...*so that they will keep Torah!*

Torah is our Kingdom duty.

Testimony of Proverbs

My son, keep thy father's commandment, and forsake not the **Torah** of thy mother:

Bind them continually upon thine heart, *and* tie them about thy neck.

When thou goest, it shall lead thee; *when* thou sleepest, it shall keep thee; and when thou awakest, it shall talk with thee.

For the commandment *is* a lamp; and the **Torah** *is* light; and reproofs of instruction *are* the way of life:

Proverbs 6.20-23

The parent loves the fence that keeps his or her child safe.
The child hates the fence because it restricts freedom.
The child becomes a parent and loves the fence.
The fence didn't change, only the attitude.
Torah's fence keeps us from traps.
Are you like parent or child?

Torah protects us from traps.

They that forsake the **Torah** praise the wicked: but such as keep the **Torah** contend with them.

Proverbs 28.4

Anti-Torah: Praise the wicked.
Pro-Torah: Fight the wicked.

Fight the wicked.
Keep Torah.

He that turneth away his ear from hearing **Torah**, even his prayer *shall be* abomination.

Proverbs 28.9

Listening to and obeying Torah puts us on "praying ground." Ignoring Torah makes prayer תּוֹעֵבָה *tow-evah* disgusting.

Without Torah we haven't got a prayer.

Where *there is* no vision, the people perish: but he that keepeth **Torah**, happy *is* he.

Proverbs 29.18

Life can be depressing.
Torah is God's antidepressant.

Who can find a [אֵשֶׁת־חַיִל] virtuous woman? for her price *is* far above rubies…

She openeth her mouth with wisdom; and in her tongue *is* the **Torah** of kindness.

Proverbs 31.10, 26

God *is* my strength *and* [חַיִל] power: and he maketh my way perfect.

2 Samuel 22.33

———————————

Most think Proverbs 31 praises a woman of purity, goodness. But the phrase אֵשֶׁת־חַיִל *eshet-chayil* is a woman soldier! חַיִל chayil is strength, might, wealth, force, and army. David said that God is his strength and chayil.

In the Tenach book order, Ruth is next after Proverbs. Proverbs asks here, "Who can find a chayil woman?" Three chapters later in Ruth 3.11 Boaz found her. All of Bethlehem recognized Ruth as chayil.

A chayil woman is a powerful force. She speaks the Torah of kindness.

Testimony of Yeshua

But he answered and said, It is written, Man shall not live by bread alone, but by every word that proceedeth out of the mouth of God.

Matthew 4.4

And he humbled thee, and suffered thee to hunger, and fed thee with manna, which thou knewest not, neither did thy fathers know; that he might make thee know that man doth not live by bread only, but by every *word* that proceedeth out of the mouth of the LORD doth man live.

Deuteronomy 8.3

Satan tempted Yeshua after Yeshua fasted forty days.
He proposed that Yeshua turn stones into bread.
Yeshua was starving, yet replied with Torah.

 Torah is food.

Jesus said unto him, It is written again, Thou shalt not tempt the Lord thy God.

Matthew 4.7

Ye shall not tempt the LORD your God, as ye tempted *him* in Massah.

Deuteronomy 6.16

For his next attack, Satan ascribed Psalm 91.11-12 to Yeshua,

"For he shall give his angels charge over thee, to keep thee in all thy ways. They shall bear thee up in *their* hands, lest thou dash thy foot against a stone."

Satan dared Yeshua to jump from the top of the Temple. Yeshua refused the dare and responded with Torah.

Torah is prudent.

Then saith Jesus unto him, Get thee hence, Satan: for it is written, Thou shalt worship the Lord thy God, and him only shalt thou serve.

Matthew 4.10

Thou shalt fear the LORD thy God, and serve him, and shalt swear by his name.

Ye shall not go after other gods, of the gods of the people which *are* round about you;

(For the LORD thy God *is* a jealous God among you) lest the anger of the LORD thy God be kindled against thee, and destroy thee from off the face of the earth.

Deuteronomy 6.13-15

Satan offered Yeshua the Kingdoms of the earth.
Yeshua rebuked Satan and then countered with Torah.

Yeshua said at the end of His earthly life, Matthew 28.18b, "All power is given unto me in heaven and in earth."

Power is ἐξουσία *exousia* power of choice,
the power of authority and of right.

Wait for God's power.
Keep Torah.

Not every one that saith unto me, Lord, Lord, shall enter into the kingdom of heaven; but he that doeth the will of my Father which is in heaven.

Many will say to me in that day, Lord, Lord, have we not prophesied in thy name? and in thy name have cast out devils? and in thy name done many wonderful works?

And then will I profess unto them, I never knew you: depart from me, ye that work iniquity.

Matthew 7.21-23

Some call Yeshua "Lord" and do spiritual things.
They think this proves relationship.
Yeshua says that it doesn't.

Words we never want to hear:
"I never knew you."

Iniquity is ἀνομία *anomia* the condition of no law, because ignorant of it, because of violating it, contempt and violation of law, iniquity, wickedness.
To which law did Yeshua refer?
Roman law? Common law?

Torah.

"No-Torah" is iniquity.

And the disciples came, and said unto him, Why speakest thou unto them in parables?

He answered and said unto them, Because it is given unto you to know the mysteries of the kingdom of heaven, but to them it is not given.

For whosoever hath, to him shall be given, and he shall have more abundance: but whosoever hath not, from him shall be taken away even that he hath.

Therefore speak I to them in parables: because they seeing see not; and hearing they hear not, neither do they understand.

And in them is fulfilled the prophecy of Esaias, which saith, By hearing ye shall hear, and shall not understand; and seeing ye shall see, and shall not perceive:

For this people's heart is waxed gross, and *their* ears are dull of hearing, and their eyes they have closed; lest at any time they should see with *their* eyes, and hear with *their* ears, and should understand with *their* heart, and should be converted, and I should heal them.

But blessed *are* your eyes, for they see: and your ears, for they hear.

Matthew 13.10-16

Yeshua spoke parables to *hide* truth, to fulfill Isaiah 6.9-10.

We can't know Torah or God's Kingdom *unless God allows.*

Master, which *is* the great commandment in the **Torah**?

Jesus said unto him, Thou shalt love the Lord thy God with all thy heart, and with all thy soul, and with all thy mind.

This is the first and great commandment.

And the second *is* like unto it, Thou shalt love thy neighbour as thyself.

On these two commandments hang all the **Torah** and the prophets.

Matthew 22.36-40

And thou shalt love the LORD thy God with all thine heart, and with all thy soul, and with all thy might.

Deuteronomy 6.5

Thou shalt not avenge, nor bear any grudge against the children of thy people, but thou shalt love thy neighbour as thyself: I *am* the LORD.

Leviticus 19.18

Yeshua summed up all of Torah in two commands.
Some think that now only those two commands count.

If traffic law could be summed up, "Everyone arrive safely," would it then be legal to speed and to run red lights?

Keep all the Torah you can.

Then spake Jesus to the multitude, and to his disciples,

Saying, The scribes and the Pharisees sit in Moses' seat:

All therefore whatsoever they bid you observe, *that* observe and do; but do not ye after their works: for they say, and do not.

Matthew 23.1-3

Pharisee authority came from Moses, which means Torah.
The church mocks Pharisees for contradicting Torah.
The church's own traditions contradict Torah.
The church should apologize to Pharisees!

Turn from unbiblical tradition.
Keep Torah.

Then the Pharisees and scribes asked him, Why walk not thy disciples according to the tradition of the elders, but eat bread with unwashen hands?

He answered and said unto them, Well hath Esaias prophesied of you hypocrites, as it is written, This people honoureth me with *their* lips, but their heart is far from me.

Howbeit in vain do they worship me, teaching *for* doctrines the commandments of men.

For laying aside the commandment of God, ye hold the tradition of men, *as* the washing of pots and cups: and many other such like things ye do.

And he said unto them, Full well ye reject the commandment of God, that ye may keep your own tradition.

Mark 7.5-9

Wherefore the Lord said, Forasmuch as this people draw near *me* with their mouth, and with their lips do honour me, but have removed their heart far from me, and their fear toward me is taught by the precept of men:

Isaiah 29.13

The Pharisees did what Isaiah warned against—
They made tradition more important than Torah.
The church also can only answer, "Guilty as charged."

Keep Torah.
Not unbiblical traditions.

Do not think that I will accuse you to the Father: there is *one* that accuseth you, *even* Moses, in whom ye trust.

For had ye believed Moses, ye would have believed me: for he wrote of me.

But if ye believe not his writings, how shall ye believe my words?

John 5.45-47

I will raise them up a Prophet from among their brethren, like unto thee, and will put my words in his mouth; and he shall speak unto them all that I shall command him.

And it shall come to pass, *that* whosoever will not hearken unto my words which he shall speak in my name, I will require *it* of him.

Deuteronomy 18.18-19

Yeshua is Torah's promised Prophet.

Torah reveals Yeshua.

Ten Commandments in the New Covenant

1. I *am* the LORD thy God, which have brought thee out of the land of Egypt, out of the house of bondage.

Exodus 20.2

The next day John seeth Jesus coming unto him, and saith, Behold the Lamb of God, which taketh away the sin of the world.

John 1.29

Purge out therefore the old leaven, that ye may be a new lump, as ye are unleavened. For even Christ our passover is sacrificed for us:

1 Corinthians 5.7

———————————————

The First Commandment: God is our Redeemer.
Through Passover, God secured our loyalty.
Yeshua is God's Passover Lamb.

Torah reveals Yeshua.

2. Thou shalt have no other gods before me.

    Thou shalt not make unto thee any graven image, or any likeness *of any thing* that *is* in heaven above, or that *is* in the earth beneath, or that *is* in the water under the earth:

    Thou shalt not bow down thyself to them, nor serve them: for I the LORD thy God *am* a jealous God, visiting the iniquity of the fathers upon the children unto the third and fourth *generation* of them that hate me;

    And shewing mercy unto thousands of them that love me, and keep my commandments.

Exodus 20.3-6

No man can serve two masters: for either he will hate the one, and love the other; or else he will hold to the one, and despise the other. Ye cannot serve God and mammon.

Matthew 6.24

Vine's says that μαμωνᾶς *mamōnas* mammon is derived from the Hebrew אָמַן *aman* be faithful, trust, believe.

Idols are traps we trust more than God.

3. Thou shalt not take the name of the LORD thy God in vain; for the LORD will not hold him guiltless that taketh his name in [שָׁוְא] vain.

Exodus 20.7

Hearken, my beloved brethren, Hath not God chosen the poor of this world rich in faith, and heirs of the kingdom which he hath promised to them that love him?

But ye have despised the poor. Do not rich men oppress you, and draw you before the judgment seats?

Do not they blaspheme that worthy name by the which ye are called?

James 2.5-7

We tend to condemn sin in rags, yet forgive sin in silk.
שָׁוְא *shahv* emptiness, vanity, lying, worthlessness
is the root of שׁוֹאָה *shoah* destruction, Holocaust.
To shahv God's Name is to try to destroy it.
It's blasphemy even when the rich do it.

 Torah keepers preserve God's Name.

4.   Remember the sabbath day, to keep it holy.

Six days shalt thou labour, and do all thy work:

But the seventh day *is* the sabbath of the LORD thy God: *in it* thou shalt not do any work, thou, nor thy son, nor thy daughter, thy manservant, nor thy maidservant, nor thy cattle, nor thy stranger that *is* within thy gates:

For *in* six days the LORD made heaven and earth, the sea, and all that in them *is*, and rested the seventh day: wherefore the LORD blessed the sabbath day, and hallowed it.

Exodus 20.8-11

And he came to Nazareth, where he had been brought up: and, as his custom was, he went into the synagogue on the sabbath day, and stood up for to read.

Luke 4.16

And Paul, as his manner was, went in unto them, and three sabbath days reasoned with them out of the scriptures,

Acts 17.2

שַׁבָּת *Shabbat* Sabbath is from שָׁבַת *shavat* cease, desist, rest. Yeshua, saints, and heroes since Moses kept the Sabbath.

Sabbath: ID badge of God's Kingdom.

5.   Honour thy father and thy mother: that thy days may be long upon the land which the LORD thy God giveth thee.

Exodus 20.12

For God commanded, saying, Honour thy father and mother: and, he that curseth his father, or his mother, shall surely be put to death.

But ye say, Whosoever shall say to *his* father or *his* mother, *It is* a gift, by whatsoever thou mightest be profited by me;

And honour not his father or his mother, *he shall be free.* Thus have ye made the commandment of God of none effect by your tradition.

Ye hypocrites, well did Esaias prophesy of you, saying,

This people draweth nigh unto me with their mouth, and honoureth me with *their* lips; but their heart is far from me.

But in vain they do worship me, teaching *for* doctrines the commandments of men.

Matthew 15.4-9

Yeshua affirmed the Commandment to honor parents. He rebuked hypocrites who put tradition over Torah.

Honoring parents extends life.

6.   Thou shalt not [רָצַח] kill.

Exodus 20.13

Ye have heard that it was said by them of old time, Thou shalt not [φονεύω] kill; and whosoever shall [φονεύω] kill shall be in danger of the judgment:

But I say unto you, That whosoever is angry with his brother without a cause shall be in danger of the judgment: and whosoever shall say to his brother, Raca, shall be in danger of the council: but whosoever shall say, Thou fool, shall be in danger of hell fire.

Matthew 5.21-22

––––––––––––––––––––

Both רָצַח *ratsach* and φονεύω *phoneuō* include murder.

Wrong anger is like murder.

7.   Thou shalt not commit adultery.

Exodus 20.14

Ye have heard that it was said by them of old time, Thou shalt not commit adultery:

But I say unto you, That whosoever looketh on a woman to lust after her hath committed adultery with her already in his heart.

Matthew 5.27-28

Marriage *is* honourable in all, and the bed undefiled: but whoremongers and adulterers God will judge.

Hebrews 13.4

———————————

"I can window shop without buying" is a lie.

Lust is adultery.

8.   Thou shalt not steal.

Exodus 20.15

Let him that stole steal no more: but rather let him labour, working with *his* hands the thing which is good, that he may have to give to him that needeth.

Ephesians 4.28

Neither repented they of their murders, nor of their sorceries, nor of their fornication, nor of their thefts.

Revelation 9.21

Torah and the New Covenant agree:

Stealing is a trap.

9.   Thou shalt not bear false witness against thy neighbour.

Exodus 20.16

Jesus said unto them, If God were your Father, ye would love me: for I proceeded forth and came from God; neither came I of myself, but he sent me.

Why do ye not understand my speech? *even* because ye cannot hear my word.

Ye are of *your* father the devil, and the lusts of your father ye will do. He was a murderer from the beginning, and abode not in the truth, because there is no truth in him. When he speaketh a lie, he speaketh of his own: for he is a liar, and the father of it.

And because I tell *you* the truth, ye believe me not.

John 8.42-45

He that overcometh shall inherit all things; and I will be his God, and he shall be my son.

But the fearful, and unbelieving, and the abominable, and murderers, and whoremongers, and sorcerers, and idolaters, and all liars, shall have their part in the lake which burneth with fire and brimstone: which is the second death.

Revelation 21.7-8

Satan is the father of lies.

Liars go to hell.

10. Thou shalt not covet thy neighbour's house, thou shalt not covet thy neighbour's wife, nor his manservant, nor his maidservant, nor his ox, nor his ass, nor any thing that *is* thy neighbour's.

Exodus 20.17

And, behold, one came and said unto him, Good Master, what good thing shall I do, that I may have eternal life?

And he said unto him, Why callest thou me good? *there is* none good but one, *that is*, God: but if thou wilt enter into life, keep the commandments.

He saith unto him, Which? Jesus said, Thou shalt do no murder, Thou shalt not commit adultery, Thou shalt not steal, Thou shalt not bear false witness,

Honour thy father and *thy* mother: and, Thou shalt love thy neighbour as thyself.

The young man saith unto him, All these things have I kept from my youth up: what lack I yet?

Jesus said unto him, If thou wilt be perfect, go *and* sell that thou hast, and give to the poor, and thou shalt have treasure in heaven: and come *and* follow me.

But when the young man heard that saying, he went away sorrowful: for he had great possessions.

Matthew 19.16-22

The rich man wanted stuff more than life.

Coveting stops life.

Testimonies of Paul, James, and John

Cursed *be* he that [קוּם] confirmeth not *all* the words of this
Torah to do them. And all the people shall say, Amen.

Deuteronomy 27.26

Do we then [καταργέω] make void the **Torah** through faith?
God forbid: yea, we establish the **Torah**.

Romans 3.31

———————————————

Cursed are all who do not קוּם *quwm* establish Torah.
Cursed are all who καταργέω *katargeō* render idle,
inactivate, cause to have no further efficiency,
deprive of force, cause to cease, put an end to,
do away with, annul, abolish, sever from,
separate from, discharge from,
loose from, or terminate all
intercourse with Torah.

Don't be cursed.
Establish Torah.

For the mystery of iniquity doth already work: only he who now letteth *will let*, until he be taken out of the way.

And then shall that Wicked be revealed, whom the Lord shall consume with the spirit of his mouth, and shall destroy with the brightness of his coming:

Even him, whose coming is after the working of Satan with all power and signs and lying wonders,

And with all deceivableness of unrighteousness in them that perish; because they received not the love of the truth, that they might be saved.

And for this cause God shall send them strong delusion, that they should believe a lie:

That they all might be damned who believed not the truth, but had pleasure in unrighteousness.

2 Thessalonians 2.7-12

———————————————

Here and in Matthew 7.23, iniquity is ἀνομία *anomia*.
Anomia is the condition of being without law.
Without which law? Torah. (Thesis 74)

Who is the Wicked, sometimes translated as the lawless one?
The Greek is ἄνομος *anomos* destitute of (the Mosaic) Law.
The Wicked, the lawless one, *is the one without Torah.*
Followers of the Wicked get a delusion from God.
They believe the lie and they are damned.

Follow Torah or be damned.

And when they had appointed him a day, there came many to him into *his* lodging; to whom he expounded and testified the kingdom of God, persuading them concerning Jesus, both out of the **Torah** of Moses, and *out of* the prophets, from morning till evening.

And some believed the things which were spoken, and some believed not.

Acts 28.23-24

At the end of Acts, Paul was under house arrest in Rome.
He argued for the Kingdom of God and Yeshua.
His proof texts were Torah and Prophets.

Jews tend to believe Torah, not Yeshua.
The church tends to believe Yeshua, not Torah.
The first to humble himself and learn from the other—wins!

Believe Torah *and* Yeshua.

But be ye doers of the word, and not hearers only, deceiving your own selves.

For if any be a hearer of the word, and not a doer, he is like unto a man beholding his natural face in a glass:

For he beholdeth himself, and goeth his way, and straightway forgetteth what manner of man he was.

But whoso looketh into the perfect **Torah** of liberty*, and continueth *therein*, he being not a forgetful hearer, but a doer of the work, this man shall be blessed in his deed.

James 1.22-25

Even so faith, if it hath not works, is dead, being alone.

James 2.17

———————————————

Martin Luther called James' letter an "epistle of straw."
He thought that James added works to salvation.
Many still believe nothing is needed after faith.
Bonhoeffer warned against this "cheap grace."

Of course you have sinned, but now everything
is forgiven, so you can stay as you are and
enjoy the consolations of forgiveness.[2]

Salvation is by faith alone,
but faith is not alone.

   Just do it.

* Thesis 45

Whosoever committeth sin transgresseth also the **Torah**: for sin is the transgression of the **Torah**.

1 John 3.4

By this we know that we love the children of God, when we love God, and keep his commandments.

For this is the love of God, that we keep his commandments: and his commandments are not grievous.

1 John 5.2-3

———————————————

Throughout the Bible, keeping Torah is loving God.
Throughout the Bible, breaking Torah is sin.

Keep Torah.
Love God.

Testimony of Revelation

And, behold, I come quickly; and my reward *is* with me, to give every man according as his work shall be.

I am Alpha and Omega, the beginning and the end, the first and the last.

Blessed *are* they that do his commandments, that they may have right to the tree of life, and may enter in through the gates into the city.

For without *are* dogs, and sorcerers, and whoremongers, and murderers, and idolaters, and whosoever loveth and maketh a lie.

Revelation 22.12-15

And I will come near to you to judgment; and I will be a swift witness against the sorcerers, and against the adulterers, and against false swearers, and against those that oppress the hireling in *his* wages, the widow, and the fatherless, and that turn aside the stranger *from his right,* and fear not me, saith the LORD of hosts.

For I *am* the LORD, I change not; therefore ye sons of Jacob are not consumed.

Malachi 3.5-6

God doesn't change.

Obey God.
Keep Torah.

Chapter 2
Torah's Calendar, Appointed Times, and Menu

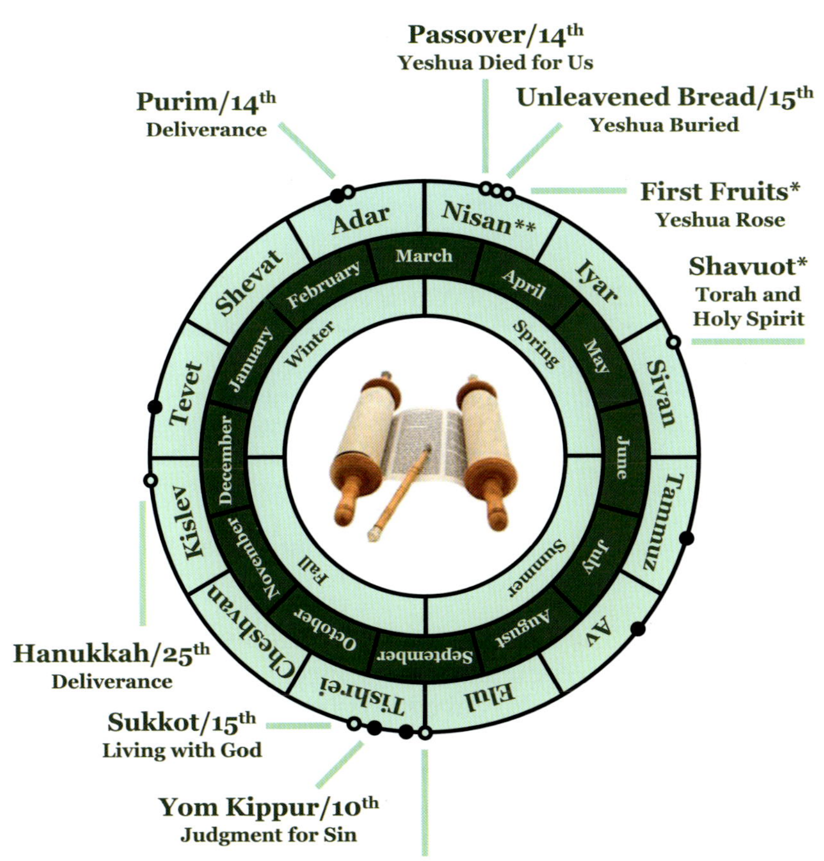

*First Fruits is the day after the Sabbath. Shavuot is the 50th day of First Fruits.
**Nisan is the 1st month of the religious year. Tishrei is the 1st of the civil year.
● Fasts: 17th of Tammuz (Golden Calf), 9th of Av (Spies' Evil Report), 3rd of Tishrei (Fast of Gadaliah), 10th of Tishrei (Yom Kippur), 10th of Tevet (Siege of Jerusalem), 13th of Adar (Fast of Esther).

Time to Act   The church ignored Torah and got lost. Let's check the Instruments and call the Control Tower. We can return to Torah's calendar, appointed times, and menu.

Calendar

Torah's calendar employs the sun and moon. Months begin on the new moon. A solar year is slightly longer than twelve lunar months, so an extra month is added seven times every nineteen years to stay in sync, Adar II. This way the four spring appointed times stay in the spring and the three fall appointed times stay in the fall.

The first month of the civil year is Tishrei. But Nisan became the first month of the religious year at the first Passover.[1] This is said to be the first command given to the nation Israel. Now Tishrei is the seventh month of the religious year.

Beginning in Genesis 1.5, days are described as evening and morning, so the biblical day begins and ends at sunset.

With this simple introduction, we can better understand God's appointed times as described in Leviticus 23.

Sabbath   The seventh day is שַׁבָּת *Shabbat* Sabbath. No work is done according to the Fourth Commandment, a perpetual covenant. So Sabbath is traditionally bookended with Candle Lighting eighteen minutes before sundown on the sixth day (Friday evening) and with *Havdalah* about forty-five minutes after Sabbath's sunset (Saturday night). Pagan names like Thursday for Thor's Day or Sunday for the sun god are avoided by naming the other days of the week first day through sixth day.

New Moon   ראֹשׁ חֹדֶשׁ *Rosh Chodesh* Head of the Month was determined by the first crescent and the Sanhedrin, but the Sanhedrin was outlawed under the reign of Theodosius. So now the new moon is determined by calculation. Numbers 10.10 says, "…in the beginnings of your months, ye shall blow with the trumpets over your burnt offerings…" Changes in liturgy replaced Temple sacrifices for this occasion, and some women's groups hold fellowship events on Rosh Chodesh.

Spring Appointed Times

Four of the seven annual appointed times are in the spring. Three occur within a week and the fourth is seven weeks later.

Passover   Yeshua commanded at פֶּסַח *Pesach* Passover in Luke 22.19-20, "This do in remembrance of me."   For Catholics this is Eucharist and for Protestants, communion. But the context is Passover, which the church replaced with Easter.[2] So for the most part today, Jews keep Passover but don't recognize Yeshua. The church recognizes Yeshua, but doesn't keep Passover. Like Mark Biltz likes to say, the first one to humble himself and learn from the other—wins!

Each home *selected a spotless lamb* on Nisan 10, *four days* before the death of Egypt's firstborn, Exodus 12.3, and *examined it for any blemish. The lamb was sacrificed on Nisan 14 and its blood smeared on the lintel and doorposts of the home.* About midnight, the Destroyer went through Egypt killing the firstborn of every home, but *passed over* any home with the *blood of the lamb*. For about 1,300 years before Yeshua, Israel celebrated a dress rehearsal for the sacrifice of *God's perfect Lamb,* 1 Corinthians 5.7, Who would set His people free from eternal death. The Destroyer *passes over* those whose *lives* are marked with the *blood of Yeshua*.

Yeshua arrived in Jerusalem *four days before Passover* with other Passover lambs. He was *examined* by the chief priests, elders, and teachers of Torah and *found to be without fault.* At the hour of the morning sacrifice, *when the Passover lamb was tied to the altar, Yeshua was nailed to the cross. Six hours later, when the Passover lamb was killed at the evening sacrifice, Yeshua died as God's perfect Passover Lamb after forgiving His enemies and saying,* "It is finished." Yeshua fulfilled Passover to the day and hour.

Passover begins the annual cycle of God's appointed times. Our relationship with God also begins with God's Lamb. By accepting Yeshua's death as a substitution for our own, Torah's death penalty is satisfied. God's Grace authorizes us live a new life in the Spirit, a life according to Torah.

Unleavened Bread　　　　　　The day after Passover, Nisan 15, begins the appointed time of חַג הַמַּצּוֹת *Chag HaMatsot* Feast of Unleavened Bread, described in Exodus 12.15-20 and Leviticus 23.6-8. The first and seventh days of Unleavened Bread are *special Sabbaths.* In preparation for the feast, *leavening is cleansed from the home and the last crumbs are wrapped in linen and removed.* Anyone who fails to remove the leaven is cut off from Israel.

When believers read John 19.31, that Yeshua was taken down and buried before the Sabbath, they often don't know about the special Sabbath which could fall on any day of the week and assume the Sabbath is "Saturday." We know that Yeshua was buried before the special Sabbath of Unleavened Bread began that evening. Yeshua promised in Matthew 12.40 that He would be in the earth for three days and three nights. We know that the women discovered Yeshua resurrected at dawn on the first day of the week, at the rising of the sun, Mark 16.2, but the text never says when He actually rose—it could have been earlier, even the evening before. The day of the crucifixion is debatable. The church's traditional day for the crucifixion, Friday, the sixth day, doesn't work—there's not enough time for Yeshua to be in the earth three days and three nights and be discovered alive on the first day. The fifth day of the week works, even the fourth, but not the sixth.

Leavening is a metaphor for sin, 1 Corinthians 5.6-8. Paul says to keep this feast *without leaven*. Peter says in 1 Peter 2.24 and Paul says in 2 Corinthians 5.21 that Yeshua, Who knew no sin/leaven, took our sin/leaven into His body when He was crucified. This changed Yeshua the Bread of Life, John 6.35, from *Bread without leaven* into *Bread with leaven* which had to be removed for the approaching appointed time of Unleavened Bread. *The disciples wrapped Yeshua in linen and hid Him away in a tomb.* When Yeshua rose from the dead, *the leaven was gone because He had destroyed sin and death.* Yeshua the Bread of Life fulfilled the Feast of Unleavened Bread. Since Yeshua destroyed sin and death, we shouldn't invite them back.

First Fruits   רֵאשִׁית *Reisheet* First Fruits is when the *first fruits* of the spring harvest were brought to the priest and *presented before the LORD.*

Paul says in 1 Corinthians 15.20-23 that Yeshua is our *Firstfruits of the resurrection,* Who *presented Himself raised from the dead.* Yeshua is the guarantee of resurrection for those whose sin has been paid for by the sacrifice of God's perfect Lamb, taken away and buried by the Bread of Life, and fully defeated because Yeshua rose from the dead.

Leviticus 23.9-14 sets this appointed time of First Fruits "on the morrow after the Sabbath." Most say that this refers to the day after the special Sabbath of Unleavened Bread, which always puts Shavuot/Pentecost on Sivan 6, any day of the week. Some say it's the day after the regular Sabbath, the first day of the week. This always puts Shavuot on the first day.

Easter is named after Ishtar/Astarte, goddess of fertility, and includes symbols of fertility: rabbits, eggs, and lilies. In contrast, Torah's appointed times celebrate what Yeshua did when He killed death, and what He will do when He returns.

Shavuot/Pentecost   Starting on "the morrow after the Sabbath," Counting the Omer in Leviticus 23.15-16 is fifty days (Πεντηκοστή *Pentēkostē* Pentecost/Fiftieth Day), or seven weeks (שָׁבֻעֹת *Shavuot* Weeks) forty-nine days plus a day, ending on Shavuot. Most in the church think that the first Pentecost happened when the disciples received the Holy Spirit in Acts 2. But as Mark Biltz likes to say, Jews kept Pentecost for about 1,300 years before Acts 2, so Jews were the first Pentecostals!

Shavuot traditionally marks the day Israel received the Ten Commandments at Mt. Sinai, when Israel said, "We do," and "married" God. God promised in Exodus 19.5-6 that Israel would be a treasure above all people, a Kingdom of priests, and a holy nation. Israel gathered in one place that morning. *Fire descended* on Mt. Sinai, Exodus 19.18-19, the *ground shook,* and the people received God's Word with *God's voice.*

Moses went up the mountain for forty days to receive the tablets. Israel sacrificed to the Golden Calf. Aaron promised in Exodus 32.5 that this sacrifice was to the LORD! God's own high priest created an appointed time, but it was a terrible sin. This is an important warning for the church, which is fond of creating feasts. God threatened to destroy Israel for the Golden Calf and to raise up a nation through Moses. But Moses argued and God repented, Exodus 32.14. Moses broke the tablets in anger when he returned to the camp and called in Exodus 32.26, "Who *is* on the LORD's side?" The Levites responded and *killed 3,000 of their brothers.*

Yeshua promised at His ascension, Acts 1.1-9, *forty days* into the Counting of the Omer, that His disciples would receive power from the Holy Spirit and they should wait in Jerusalem. They would know Yeshua meant Shavuot, the mandatory pilgrimage just ten days later. So on Shavuot, the disciples gathered in the House, a synonym for the Temple, Isaiah 56.7. *Fire descended* on their heads. They were filled with the Holy Spirit and *praised God in tongues,* heard by Jews gathered from all over the world in their own languages. *Jerusalem shook* with these signs. *About 3,000 Jewish brothers received life* that day. 5,000 more in Acts 4.4 and even more in Acts 6.7. By Acts 21.20, tens of thousands of Jews believed in Yeshua, all zealous for Torah.

Shavuot is the celebration of receiving Torah and the Spirit. Torah, Yeshua, and the Holy Spirit are all in agreement.

Fall Appointed Times

Yeshua the Lamb fulfilled the spring appointed times at His first coming. Yeshua the Lion will fulfill the fall appointed times at His second coming. These last three are called the High Holy Days and occur in Tishrei, September or October.

Trumpets   Trumpets is also called יוֹם תְּרוּעָה *Yom Teruah* Day of Blowing. It falls on Tishrei 1 and is a special Sabbath. Teruah can mean signal, shout, blast of war, alarm, or joy. Another name is רֹאשׁ הַשָּׁנָה *Rosh Hashanah* Head of the Year, since Tishrei is the first month of the civil calendar and Tishrei 1 begins the civil New Year. Trumpets in tradition celebrates a break from harvesting and the beginning of the ten Days of Awe. It was often the day of *coronation for a king*. And it marks the *opening of the Books of Judgment*. On Tishrei 10, Yom Kippur, the Books are closed for another year.

Paul wrote in 1 Thessalonians 4.16-17, "For the Lord himself shall descend from heaven with a shout, with the voice of the archangel, and with the trump of God: and the dead in Christ shall rise first: Then we which are alive and remain shall be caught up together with them in the clouds, to meet the Lord in the air: and so shall we ever be with the Lord."

On Trumpets, the last of 100 blasts of the *shofar* or ram's horn is known as the "last trump." Again, in 1 Corinthians 15.52, "In a moment, in the twinkling of an eye, at the last trump: for the trumpet shall sound, and the dead shall be raised incorruptible, and we shall be changed." We don't know the day of the week, the hour, or the year, Matthew 24.36-39. But that doesn't mean we have to be caught off guard, as Paul says in 1 Thessalonians 5.4, "But ye, brethren, are not in darkness, that that day should overtake you as a thief." A future Trumpets is the next appointed time for Yeshua to fulfill.

Psalm 89.15, "Blessed is the people that know the [teruah] joyful sound: they shall walk, O LORD, in the light of thy countenance." By celebrating Trumpets, we learn to recognize *the day of Yeshua's coronation, the sound of alarm for war and joy, the day the Books are opened and judgment begins.*

Yom Kippur   יוֹם כִּפּוּר *Yom Kippur* Day of Atonement is Tishrei 10, another special Sabbath. Leviticus 23.27-32 says that anyone who works or fails to afflict his soul this day is to be cut off from his people. Fasting is a way to afflict the soul and Paul refers to this day as "the fast" in Acts 27.9.

Yom Kippur is the only day of the year when the high priest entered the Most Holy Place. He wore only the standard priest's linen garments for this duty, Leviticus 16.4, not the high priest's gold plate on his forehead, the ephod, the breastplate, or the colored robe with bells and pomegranates. *He sprinkled the blood of sacrifice on the Mercy Seat,* the Ark's cover, to make atonement. The root of atonement is כָּפַר *kaphar* cover, ransom, and is also the pitch which sealed Noah's ark inside and out. After the sin of the Golden Calf, Moses went back up Mt. Sinai. Yom Kippur is the traditional day Moses returned from Mt. Sinai with new tablets. With these new tablets, God showed that He was still keeping covenant with Israel despite their sin with the Golden Calf. The earthly Tabernacle is a copy of the one in heaven. Hebrews 9 says that *Yeshua perfected this sacrifice* [Yom Kippur] *when He offered His own blood on the Mercy Seat of the Tabernacle in heaven.*

Revelation 19.11-21 recalls Isaiah 63.1-6—Yeshua is King of Kings and Lord of Lords Whose Name is The Word of God. His robe is dipped in blood as He treads the *winepress* of the fury of God, accompanied by the army of heaven *clothed in fine, white linen.* For Jews in the early church, *white linen would remind them both of the high priest's garments worn on Yom Kippur, and the kittel, a white linen burial garment without pockets* (you can send treasure ahead, Matthew 6.20, but you can't take any treasure with you), *which males wear on Yom Kippur* and a few other times. *Grapes* are a late crop, another reference to the fall feasts.

God's judgment will be joy for the righteous and suffering for the wicked. Observing Yom Kippur is a sobering way to prepare for that solemn day.

Tabernacles   Torah's last annual appointed time is סֻכּוֹת *Sukkot* Tabernacles/Booths, described in Leviticus 23.33 to the end of the chapter. Tishrei 15 is a special Sabbath. For seven days there are waving of the four species, *water celebrations,* and *living in temporary structures* called sukkahs or booths. Tabernacles recalls God's protection of Israel in the wilderness and looks forward to living with God.

In Exodus 25.8-9, God said that the Tabernacle would allow Him to live with Israel. John 1.14a says, "And the Word was made flesh, and [σκηνόω *skēnoō* tabernacled] among us." *Living in a temporary dwelling reminds us that God humbled Himself to live with Israel, Yeshua humbled Himself to live in a physical body,* Philippians 2.5-11, *and our bodies are temporary tabernacles,* 2 Peter 1.13-14.

שְׁמִינִי עֲצֶרֶת *Shemini Atzaret* Eighth Day of Assembly is a special Sabbath named by the Hebrew of Leviticus 23.36. שִׂמְחַת תּוֹרָה *Simchat Torah* Rejoicing of Torah is an added celebration to mark the completion of the year's Torah-reading cycle. The scroll is unrolled, various sections are read, and the scroll is rerolled to renew the cycle in Genesis, accompanied by much singing and dancing.

Tenach's three divisions refer to Tabernacles and Yeshua:

Torah, Exodus 15.2, "The LORD *is* my strength and song, and he is become my [יְשׁוּעָה *yeshua*] salvation: he *is* my God, and I will prepare him an habitation; my father's God, and I will exalt him."

Nevi'im/Prophets, Isaiah 12.2-3, "Behold, God *is* my יְשׁוּעָה; I will trust, and not be afraid: for the LORD JEHOVAH *is* my strength and *my* song; he also is become my יְשׁוּעָה. Therefore with joy shall ye draw water out of the wells of יְשׁוּעָה."

Ketuvim/Writings, Psalm 118.14-15, "The LORD *is* my strength and song, and is become my יְשׁוּעָה. The voice of rejoicing and יְשׁוּעָה *is* in the tabernacles of the righteous: the right hand of the LORD doeth valiantly."

Yeshua announced in John 7.37b-38 in reference to the *water celebration* and Isaiah 12.3, 6, "If any man thirst, let him come unto me, and drink. He that believeth on me, as the scripture hath said, out of his belly shall flow rivers of living water." Yeshua is *Living Water* from heaven, yet He was rejected by many. Jeremiah 2.12-13, "Be astonished, O ye heavens, at this, and be horribly afraid, be ye very desolate, saith the LORD. For my people have committed two evils; they have forsaken me the fountain of living waters, *and* hewed them out cisterns, broken cisterns, that can hold no water."

Four huge *lamps* high above the Temple court burned throughout Tabernacles, lighting the city. At festival's end, *the nights went dark again.* The day after the festival, Yeshua announced in John 8.12, "I am the light of the world: he that followeth me shall not walk in darkness, but shall have the light of life." In John 9, Yeshua proved this by healing a blind man.

Tabernacles was largely neglected until Nehemiah's time, Nehemiah 8.17, when it was revived after almost 1,000 years. After Yeshua returns to the Mount of Olives, Zechariah 14.4, verses 16-19 say that all the nations who fought against Israel will celebrate Tabernacles in Jerusalem every year. Any nation not represented at the feast gets plague and drought.

The International Christian Embassy in Jerusalem says,

> The Feast of Tabernacles is always a wonderful foretaste of that future time when all peoples will come up to Jerusalem to celebrate Sukkot. It is a prophetic statement that our Lord is indeed coming soon. And it declares to Israel and the nations that a new day is dawning. The King is coming, and we are here to rejoice in His transforming power and soon arrival. It is also a time to stand with Israel and assure them that the God Who delivered them out of Egypt will also deliver them today. The God of Israel will come and tabernacle with His people.

Other Appointed Times

Purim   פּוּרִים *Purim* begins in the Book of Esther and tells of the salvation of Israel throughout the vast Persian Empire, 127 provinces from Ethiopia to India. Evil Haman, a vizier of King Ahasuerus, detested the Jews and crafted a plan to destroy them. He set the date for their destruction by casting the פּוּר *pur* lot, source of the name Purim, and came up with Adar 13, last month of the biblical year. Anticipating this date, enemies of the Jews made themselves known. Imagine their taunts, knowing they would enjoy an empire-wide pogrom, killing and looting all the Jews! But God knows the end from the beginning. Haman was outwitted by Esther, the secretly Jewish queen, and her uncle Mordechai. The date of extermination became a day of salvation. Esther 9.26-32 declares Adar 14 a day of celebration forever.

We can discover the spring of Haman's bitter hatred. Esau hated Jacob and promised to kill him for getting their father Isaac's blessing, Genesis 27.41. Esau's grandson Amalek, Genesis 36.12, carried that offense. Amalekites attacked Israel in the wilderness, Exodus 17.8-16. Deuteronomy 25.18 says that Amalek H7136 קָרָה *qarah* happened upon Israel. Amalek had no fear of God and struck the weak when the opportunity presented itself, but Israel fears God and protects the weak, so Amalek and Israel will always be in conflict.

Or the verse could be read that Amalek H7135 קָרָה *qarah* chilled Israel. Terrorist Amalek struck the weak in order to freeze the strong. Either way, God commanded Israel to *remember to blot out the memory of Amalek.*

In Judges 3.12-13, Eglon king of Moab strengthened and united with Amalek to defeat Israel, but later God raised up Judge Ehud to kill Eglon. Judge Gideon defeated Midianites and Amalekites in Judges 6-7. Gideon won partly because his terrorist enemies all distrusted each other. King Saul, *son of Kish,* refused to kill King Agag of the Amalekites, so the prophet Samuel himself killed Agag in 1 Samuel 15. Samuel told Saul that obedience is better than sacrifice, and Saul's kingdom was torn from him for his failure to kill Agag. Israel took land from Amalek in 1 Chronicles 4.39-43 and 500 men of Simeon killed the remainder of Amalek there.

Haman was descended from King Agag, Esther 3.1, therefore *Haman was an Amalekite.* Incensed that Mordechai the Jew, a *son of Kish,* Esther 2.5, wouldn't bow to him, Haman wanted to finish the job begun by his ancestors. The 1000-year-old battle between Amalek and Israel and the 500-year-old battle between *King Agag and a son of Kish* was fought again. Another decisive victory for Israel.

The Book of Esther is the only book of the Bible in which God is never mentioned. This has been described as a literary device: since God's hand behind the scenes is so clear, omitting references to God highlights His role. God is working—even when we don't see or hear Him.

Generation to generation, other "Amalekites" have risen to destroy Israel. The church developed Replacement Theology to justify killing Jews. Luther endorsed Amalek in the sixteenth century. Hitler acted on Luther's advice in the twentieth century. Hitler made anti-Semitism unpopular, so today few in the West will admit to hating Jews. They say instead that the nation of Israel is illegal and apartheid. Simply studying history and visiting Israel will prove these accusations untrue. But for those who hate Israel, truth is not the goal. As believers, we should seek truth.

"Amalek" in the Middle East, however, is candid about his desire to destroy Israel. Iran threatens continually, as in 2008, "...the Zionist regime has reached a total dead end. Thanks to god, your wish will soon be realized, and this germ of corruption will be wiped off."[3] חָמָס *chamas* Hamas, violence, cruelty, injustice, promises to make "Palestine" what Nazis called *Judenfrei,* free of Jews. ISIL declares itself the Islamic State of Syria and the Levant, an area that includes Israel. America joins Israel's enemies in calling for the "Two-State Solution" and a return to "Pre-1967 borders." Israel would experience sudden genocide if it ever agreed.

Celebrating Purim is a fun way to show support for Israel while reminding ourselves of the duty to destroy Amalek.

Hanukkah The Feast of חֲנֻכָּה *Hanukkah* Dedication celebrates the Jews' victory over the Greeks who tried to destroy Judaism. About 350 years before Yeshua, Alexander the Great conquered the known world. Israel feared his advance. But as Josephus relates in his *Antiquities,* Jaddua the high priest had a dream from God and met Alexander dressed in his high priest's robes. To everyone's surprise, Alexander saluted Jaddua. When asked why he did that, Alexander explained that he was honoring God Who had given him a dream of success and meeting this priest. Jaddua showed Alexander texts from the prophet Daniel which fit Alexander's defeat of Persia. Alexander favored the Jews. But other Greek kings after Alexander weren't so cordial.

When the Ptolemy king of Egypt and the Seleucid king of Syria fought, Israel was caught in the middle. In 168 BC, Antiochus *Epiphanes* God Manifest attacked Egypt, but Egypt had a new ally in Rome. The Roman consul drew a circle around Antiochus and ordered him to decide before he stepped outside the circle if he would leave peaceably. The one the Jews called *Epimanes* Madman submitted, left Egypt, and stormed into Israel in a rage. He enforced Hellenization, assimilation to Greek culture. Circumcision and Sabbath were outlawed. The Temple was desecrated with a statue of Zeus. On Kislev 25, a pig was sacrificed on the altar. Faithful Jews were killed for resisting assimilation to Greek culture.

Greeks came to Modin, home of the priest Mattityahu, to enforce the sacrifice of a pig. But Mattityahu and his sons killed the Greek emissaries plus the Jew who offered to make the sacrifice. They fled into the mountains and were joined by other zealots. 1 Maccabees 3.16-22 describes how Judah/Yehuda, son of Mattityahu, encouraged his men that, since they fought for God, God would win the war for them. This unlikely band defeated the powerful Greek army, the first miracle of Hanukkah. They rededicated the Temple on Kislev 25, the third anniversary of its desecration.

Jews were threatened with annihilation at Purim. But at Hanukkah, Jews faced assimilation. Even today, many consider assimilation worse than death. Yeshua kept Hanukkah, John 10.22-23. In Matthew 24.15-28, Yeshua warned that believers would face another event like Hanukkah with suffering, war, and the threat of assimilation.

The second major miracle of Hanukkah is that, though only one day's worth of sanctified oil was found, it burned in the Temple menorah for eight days until new oil was available. This event was commemorated the next year and ever since.

The Miracle of the Oil is a clue to the character God seeks. At the Burning Bush in Exodus 3.3, Moses wondered מַדּוּעַ *maduah* why the bush wasn't consumed. Maduah looks back at the cause. Maduah could be expressed as, "What do you know?" Science is מַדָּע *madah*. Moses' investigation led to meeting God. And Moses was also a fighter. He defended a Hebrew slave from an Egyptian's beating.   He defended Jethro's daughters from shepherds. In both cases, he could have looked away. Moses even "wrestled" with God. After the Golden Calf, when God was ready to destroy all of Israel, Moses challenged God in Exodus 32.11, "...[לָמָה *lamah*] why doth thy wrath wax hot against thy people…?" and in verse 12, "[Lamah] should the Egyptians speak and say…?" Lamah looks forward and literally means "to what?" "What is the purpose?" After Moses' stubborn challenging of God, God repented. God wants faithful men and women who will seek, seek, wrestle with Him, and ask, "Why?"

David Fohrman, who explains this in Aleph Beta Academy, says that even though God didn't overtly defeat the Greeks, God was always at work. Then God winked at Israel with the Miracle of the Oil. When we light our Hanukkah candles, we wink back. Even when God is silent, we are not alone.

Like Passover and Purim, Hanukkah celebrates, "They tried to kill us, God saved us, let's eat!" Latkes, which are potato pancakes, and donuts, both fried in oil, are among the special treats. !חַג שָׂמֵחַ *Chag Sa'me'ach!* Happy Holiday!

Sabbath Year   Every seventh year is a שְׁמִטָּה *Shemitah* Year of Release, Sabbath year, no sowing or reaping allowed. After seven Shemitahs, the fiftieth year is the יוֹבֵל *Yovel* Jubilee. These are all described in Leviticus 25.

What about food when there's no sowing or reaping? Verses 20-22 address this concern. God promises a triple blessing in the sixth year to provide food for three years.

2 Chronicles 36.20-21 explains that the exile to Babylon was punishment for ignoring the Sabbath year during the previous 490 years. Seventy years of exile allowed the Land to recover its lost Sabbaths. "And them that had escaped from the sword carried he away to Babylon; where they were servants to him and his sons until the reign of the kingdom of Persia: To fulfil the word of the LORD by the mouth of Jeremiah, until the land had enjoyed her sabbaths: *for* as long as she lay desolate she kept sabbath, to fulfil threescore and ten years."

Today in Israel some farmers rest in the Shemitah. There are anecdotal stories about how God blesses them for it.

The civil New Year begins in the fall on Tishrei 1, Trumpets or Rosh Hashanah.   Fall 2015 ends Sabbath year 5775 and begins a new seven-year cycle on Trumpets. If a year is evenly divisible by seven like 5775, it is traditionally understood to be a Sabbath year.   By this reckoning, the previous two Sabbath years ended in the fall of 2001 (5761) and the fall of 2008 (5768). This is interesting because of what happened at the ends of those Sabbath years.

Debts and slaves are to be released in the Sabbath year. The last date to release debts is Elul 29, the last day of the civil year, the last day before Trumpets. Jonathan Cahn, author of *The Harbinger* and *The Mystery of the Shemitah,* shows that two of the three largest stock market drops in American history each occurred on Elul 29 in 2001 and Elul 29 in 2008 respectively. As I write, it remains to be seen if something similar will happen near Elul 29 at the end of Sabbath year 5775. That day is Sunday, September 13, 2015.

Year of Jubilee   The description for יוֹבֵל *Yovel* Jubilee begins in Leviticus 25.8. The Year of Jubilee allows Land to return to its original owner under certain conditions. In this way, the Land is never permanently owned by anyone other than God and property returns to the one who may have sold it because of poverty. Words from verse ten are inscribed on America's Liberty Bell, "…Proclaim liberty throughout *all* the land unto all the inhabitants thereof…"

As the world pressures Israel to trade Land for peace, Leviticus 25.23 stands in opposition. Observant Israel understands that the Land which belongs to God, and which God dedicated in Genesis to Abraham, Isaac, Jacob/Israel, and Israel's descendants, may never be given to those who obey different commandments and worship a different god.

Judah ben Samuel wrote down a 500-year prophecy about Jerusalem and the Jubilee in 1217 AD,

> When the Ottomans conquer Jerusalem they will rule over Jerusalem for eight jubilees. Afterwards Jerusalem will become no-man's land for one jubilee, and then in the ninth jubilee it will once again come back into the possession of the Jewish nation – which would signify the beginning of the Messianic end time.[4]

300 years after he wrote this prophecy, Ottomans conquered Jerusalem in 1517 AD and held it for exactly 400 years and eight Jubilees until 1917. That's when General Allenby of the British drove out the Ottoman Turks. Confusion followed for the next fifty years: the British, the League of Nations, and then Jordan after Israel's 1948 War of Independence controlled Jerusalem. But during the 6-Day War of 1967, Israel regained Jerusalem for the first time in almost 2,000 years and they've held it since. The last fifty years, the last Jubilee in this prophecy, ends in 2017. Over 99% of Judah ben Samuel's 500-year prophecy has been fulfilled!

The church may have forgotten Torah's calendar and appointed times, but God and Israel have not.

Torah's Menu

Most in the church think that Leviticus 11's menu no longer applies. They think the reason is Acts 10. Peter received a vision of a large sheet full of various animals lowered down to him. God commanded Peter to kill and eat. Recognizing some animals as unclean, Peter refused, since he had never eaten anything common or unclean. Peter's vision is discussed again in more detail in Chapter 3 under the heading, *Didn't God Show Peter that All Foods are Clean?*

It's interesting that, while most in the church believe that Peter's vision canceled the food laws of Leviticus 11, Peter himself interpreted his own vision to mean that he should not call any *man* common or unclean, Acts 10.28. In chapter 11, the disciples got the same message from Peter's vision. No one except Gentiles got any message concerning food.

It's also interesting that while some in the church understand that Peter's vision was about Gentiles and not food, they still think that the food laws of Leviticus 11 are annulled. They fall back on Yeshua's statements which are also addressed in Chapter 3 under *Didn't Yeshua Declare All Foods Clean?* A sensible question to ask at this point is, "How long after Yeshua's death and resurrection did Peter have this vision?" Various commentaries put it at a few years to ten or more. Peter lived with, studied under, and ate with Yeshua. Yet years later Peter still refused a command from God to eat unclean animals, saying that he had never done so and he wouldn't now? Peter never got Yeshua's memo that all foods had been declared clean!

Since Leviticus 11 still stands, what are these food restrictions? Only clean or unclean animals as found in Leviticus 11 are addressed here. Kosher has a multitude of additional regulations. One can eat clean without much trouble, but eating kosher is considerably more difficult.

A general rule is not to eat meat with blood in it, as commanded as early as Genesis 9.4 and again in Leviticus 19.26. Meat certified as kosher is one way to avoid blood.

Clean Food   Leviticus 11 describes clean and unclean animals, whether beast, fish, or bird. A vegetarian menu is necessarily clean. Common is another issue, as certain foods such as meat or wine, even if clean, could be made common by being offered to an idol or being handled improperly. Food made common in this way is prohibited by Acts 15 at the Jerusalem Council along with blood, the meat of strangled animals, and sexual immorality.

Clean Beasts   To be clean, a beast must chew the cud and have a cloven hoof. Cows, sheep, and goats are the animals we normally think of, but there are others. Leviticus gives examples of animals that have only one of the two qualifications. The hare chews the cud, but it has no split hoof, so it is unclean. People used to mock the Bible for saying that the hare chews the cud. Then then it turned out the hare actually does chew the cud, though in a rather unappealing way. The pig has a split hoof, but does not chew the cud, so it is unclean. Leviticus 11.8 prohibits even touching the carcass of a pig. This is difficult, since there is a saying in the industry, "We use everything but the squeal!" Products made from pigs can be found in fabric softeners, paint, and candles. Many foods such as yogurt, muffin mix, or candy may contain porcine gelatin or lard. If you like s'mores around the campfire, don't worry, you can buy kosher marshmallows. And if you long for bacon, turkey bacon might do it for you.

Clean Fish   Clean fish have both fins and scales. Once on a fishing charter, I caught more lingcod than anyone else, but I couldn't see any scales, so I gave them all away. Back on land, I went to a kosher site and saw that lingcod have very small scales and are clean. Clams, oysters, and crabs are all unclean. Lobster tastes great with butter, but it's an ocean scavenger which has neither fins nor scales.

Clean Birds   Ducks, geese, and chickens are clean, among others. Leviticus gives examples of birds which are unclean, such as the vulture, owl, and heron.

New Menu   Eating clean is easy. *L'chaim!*

Fast Days   The four fast days of Zechariah 8.19 all relate to the destruction of the first Temple and sometimes also the second Temple. Fasts are usually kept by abstaining from food and drink from dawn until dark, but Tisha B'Av and Yom Kippur are more solemn and have special rules.

Fourth Month   Tammuz is the fourth month and Tammuz 17 marks Moses smashing the tablets because of the sin of the Golden Calf. The daily sacrifice ceased this day during Nebuchadnezzar's siege. Also on this day, the Romans breached the walls of Jerusalem. Three weeks later on the Ninth of Av the Romans destroyed the Temple. The three weeks between the two fasts are called the Dire Straits.

Fifth Month   תִּשְׁעָה בְּאָב *Tisha B'Av* Ninth of Av is the worst day in Israel's history, beginning when the spies gave the evil report about the Land and Israel spent forty years in the wilderness. Many other calamities have befallen the Jewish people on this day, including the destruction of both the first and second Temples.

Seventh Month   Tishrei 3, the Fast of Gedaliah, laments the assassination of Gedaliah, the Jewish governor after Nebuchadnezzar's destruction of Jerusalem. After Gedaliah's death, the Jews of Jerusalem fled to Egypt.

Tenth Month   On Tevet 10, Nebuchadnezzar's army laid siege to Jerusalem. This war ended with Judah's seventy-year exile to Babylon.

Other Fast Days   Yom Kippur/Day of Atonement is Tishrei 10. Anyone who works or who does not afflict his soul on this day is cut off from Israel, Leviticus 23.26-32.

Adar 13 is the Fast of Esther, the date chosen by evil Haman to destroy all the Jews of Persia. The day of terror became a day of salvation. After fasting, Adar 14 is the Feast of Purim.

When asked in Matthew 9.14-15 why His disciples didn't fast, Yeshua said that after His departure His disciples would fast. One day, Zechariah said, these fast days will become feast days. But for now, we should join Israel in fasting.

Chapter 3
Traditional Objections to Torah

Witnesses for Torah

We've seen that Abraham, Moses, Joshua, David, Hosea, Amos, Micah, Isaiah, Josiah, Zephaniah, Jeremiah, Daniel, Ezekiel, Ezra, Nehemiah, Zechariah, Malachi, the authors of Psalms, Proverbs, Kings, and Hebrews, plus Yeshua, James, Paul, and John all testified for Torah. Keeping Torah brings blessings and life. Breaking Torah brings curses and death.

Witnesses against Torah

When believers begin to seek Torah, someone in the church will warn that they are putting themselves under the Law and they will have to keep all the Law perfectly or lose salvation. *But the church doesn't know the Bible's definition of its own covenant, Torah written in the heart, so it falls for these traditional objections to Torah.* When the Prodigal Son in Luke 15.11-32 repented and returned home, his Father ran to meet him, kissed him, clothed him, and celebrated, "For this my son was dead, and is alive again; he was lost, and is found." How strange then that the church would throw objections and threats at a wandering Gentile who seeks Torah obedience!

Isn't Keeping Torah another Gospel?

Galatians is often quoted to show the error of seeking Torah. So let's take another look, this time keeping a bright line in mind. On one side of the bright line is salvation by Grace. On the other side of the bright line is sanctification through Torah obedience, perfected and illustrated by Yeshua.

1.8　　"But though we, or an angel from heaven, preach any other gospel unto you than that which we have preached unto you, let him be accursed." Paul consistently teaches salvation by Grace, through faith. Torah seekers believe *this* Gospel.

2.16　　"…not justified by the works of **Torah**." Agreed.

3.10　　"...Cursed *is* every one that continueth not in all things which are written in the book of the **Torah** to do them." Paul addresses those who trust in works, not Grace, for salvation.

3.13　　"Christ hath redeemed us from the curse of the **Torah**." Yeshua destroyed Torah's curse. Now we can seek Torah, fail, and not die. We already died! Now we're free to have Torah written on our heart, one of the goals of the New Covenant.

3.21　　"*Is* the **Torah** then against the promises of God? God forbid:" Paul agrees that Torah is *not* against God's promises.

5.4　　"Christ is become of no effect unto you, whosoever of you are justified by the **Torah**; ye are fallen from grace." Torah seekers are not trusting in works. Justification is by Grace, through faith in Yeshua's death to pay the penalty for our sin.

5.16ff.　Paul lists violations of Torah from a Matthew 5.21-48 perspective. All of these violations rob us of life in the Spirit.

6.14　　"…God forbid that I should glory, save in the cross…" Salvation is because of what Yeshua did. Not what we do.

Where is the alleged anti-Torah bias? 5.21 says that if we practice works of the flesh, we won't inherit God's Kingdom. The church hid Torah's foundation and treasures with its traditional objections. But now we can winnow through the confusion and let God's Spirit blow away tradition's chaff. The experts are wrong.

Standard Objections

Here are three standard objections regularly directed at Torah seekers, followed by Mark Biltz's responses:

1. Torah seekers try to earn salvation through Torah.
2. Torah can't even be kept today.
3. God canceled Torah.

1. "Get to work!"   Torah doesn't replace salvation by Grace through faith. To see why, imagine our kitchen.

We require our children to wash the dishes. If a neighbor child washed our dishes, we might appreciate it. But if that child thought that by coming over every day to wash the dishes and to do other chores he or she would become a member of our family, we would have to correct the misunderstanding. There are only two ways to join our family: birth or adoption. No amount of "works" makes someone a member. But once in our family, as all our children know, there is work to do.

In the same way, keeping Torah will not earn anyone a place in God's family. But once in God's family, there is work to do. Salvation is by faith alone. But faith is not alone.

2. "Do what you can!"   Although today there is no Temple, priesthood, or sacrifices, other commandments can still be kept.

Imagine a Mom who gives her child three chores to do while she runs errands: wash the dishes, do a load of laundry, and vacuum the floors. The first chore the child picks is vacuuming. But the vacuum is broken. When Mom gets home, nothing is done. "Why are none of the chores done?" Mom asks. "Because the vacuum is broken!" retorts the child. Frustrated with the child's laziness, Mom explains, "Even though the vacuum is broken, you still should have washed the dishes and done a load of laundry!"

We can't do all of Torah, but there's plenty we can do.

3. "Keep your gifts!"   In Isaiah 1.11-17 and 1 Samuel 15.22, God says that He doesn't want sacrifices, the very sacrifices He commanded in Torah. Did God cancel Torah?

Imagine a man who cheats on his wife. Feeling guilty, he grabs a bouquet of flowers on his way home. But his wife throws the flowers back at him! Does his wife want flowers or a faithful husband? Flowers from a faithful husband are appreciated; a bribe from a cheating man is not.

God designed his system of sacrifices as a way to draw closer. In fact, the Hebrew words for approach, relative, and sacrifice all share the same root, קָרַב *qarav*. When we sacrifice, we draw closer to the object of our sacrifice. But if the person offering the sacrifice is unrepentant and hopes to manipulate God by offering a bribe, that "gift" is just a slap in the face.

God hates bribes, not Torah.

Didn't Yeshua Declare All Foods Clean?

Mark 7.18-19 And he saith unto them, Are ye so without understanding also? Do ye not perceive, that whatsoever thing from without entereth into the man, *it* cannot defile him; Because it entereth not into his heart, but into the belly, and goeth out into the draught, purging all meats? [Other versions end with something like, "Thus he declared all foods clean."]

If Yeshua declared all foods clean, Leviticus 11 is annulled. According to Deuteronomy 13, that makes Yeshua a false prophet Who tried to get Israel to break Torah. If on the other hand it's the church who changed Torah, then the church did the very thing which most upset Yeshua concerning the Pharisees—it put tradition over Torah. God says that He uses these situations to test Israel, to see if Israel loves Him with a whole heart. Peter never understood from living with, eating with, and listening to Yeshua that Leviticus 11 was annulled, as demonstrated in Acts 10. He just kept eating clean food and he even balked at a vision from heaven to do otherwise. So what did Yeshua mean?

Let's take another look at Mark 7.1-23 and the similar passage in Matthew 15.1-20. Solving one solves the other.

The context in both passages is a hand washing tradition, not unclean food. The Pharisees were upset that Yeshua allowed His disciples to break tradition. Many people think when reading this passage that there must be a Torah command to wash hands, but there is not. Only in the oral tradition are there commands concerning hand washing. In keeping with Torah's preeminence which He expressed in Matthew 5.17-19, Yeshua quoted Isaiah on how bad it is to void Torah with tradition. Then He gave an example how the Pharisees voided the command to honor parents. Yeshua concluded by saying that nothing that enters a man's stomach makes him κοινόω *koinoō* common, the word used in both Matthew 15.20 and Mark 7.15. But the things that come out of the heart do make a man common.

What does Yeshua mean that food goes in and out and doesn't make a man common? Let's say I ate a meal at a restaurant not knowing it had been offered to an idol, which is possible. There was no intent to sin. It's like swallowing a bug: I didn't want to do it, it was gross, now it's over, and no one blames me for it. But if I choose to eat food sacrificed to an idol, that's evil intent. The real issue is my heart, not my food. The disciples ate without washing their hands and broke oral tradition, not Torah. So what? Yeshua is making two points:

    1. Motives of the heart are more important than food.
    2. Stop putting man's tradition over God's Torah.

Some versions say, "Thus he declared all foods clean." The words "Thus he declared" aren't in the original. That leaves "purging all meats" in the KJV vs. "all foods clean" in other versions, which depends on how καθαρίζω *katharizō* to clean/cleanse is translated. The KJV sticks with the context: food comes in and food goes out, "purging all meats." Food comes and goes, but motives of the heart stick.

Yeshua didn't break Torah and declare all foods clean.

Didn't God Show Peter that All Foods are Clean?

Acts 10.9b-16   …Peter went up upon the housetop to pray about the sixth hour: And he became very hungry, and would have eaten: but while they made ready, he fell into a trance, And saw heaven opened, and a certain vessel descending unto him, as it had been a great sheet knit at the four corners, and let down to the earth: Wherein were all manner of fourfooted beasts of the earth, and wild beasts, and creeping things, and fowls of the air. And there came a voice to him, Rise, Peter; kill, and eat. But Peter said, Not so, Lord; for I have never eaten any thing that is common or unclean. And the voice *spake* unto him again the second time, What God hath cleansed, *that* call not thou common. This was done thrice: and the vessel was received up again into heaven.

Understandably, it seems that Leviticus 11 is canceled—Peter was told three times to eat unclean animals. But consider:

First, this event took place some years after Yeshua's earthly ministry. All that time, Peter never understood that Leviticus 11 was canceled. He continued to eat only clean food.

Second, a general rule of Bible interpretation is to let the Bible interpret itself if it is doing that. Peter interpreted his own vision at Cornelius' home, verse 28b, "God hath shewed me that I should not call any man common or unclean." If we're steeped in church tradition, we want to say, "Peter, God was showing you that no *food* is unclean! Don't you get it? God wasn't talking about men!" But Peter made a doctrine of this revelation in verse 34, "Then Peter opened his mouth, and said, Of a truth I perceive that God is no respecter of persons."

A dream about food can mean something else. Joseph dreamed of sheaves of grain bowing down to him in Genesis 37.7-8. His brothers knew that they were the sheaves who would bow down to Joseph. In Judges 7.12-15, Gideon and two of his enemies understood that a dream about a barley loaf smashing tents was really Gideon's sword.

Peter repeated the lesson in Acts 11, when he was challenged by believers of the circumcision sect for going to the Gentiles. Verse 18 records, "When they heard these things, they held their peace, and glorified God, saying, Then hath God also to the Gentiles granted repentance unto life." Peter repeated his lesson again in Acts 15.7-11 at the Jerusalem Council.

All the Jewish believers, even the circumcision sect, the least likely to accept Gentiles, got the message from Peter's vision that God was accepting Gentiles. No one except the Gentile church took away any lesson from this vision concerning food. After nearly 2,000 years, we can finally get it right too: Leviticus 11 is still God's menu.

Didn't James Require Just Four Laws?

Acts 15.19-20   Wherefore my sentence is, that we trouble not them, which from among the Gentiles are turned to God: But that we write unto them, that they abstain from pollutions of idols, and *from* fornication, and *from* things strangled, and *from* blood.

Paul and Barnabas returned to Jerusalem after seeing many Gentiles put faith in Yeshua. But some in Jerusalem insisted that Gentiles would be accepted only if they were first circumcised. The Jerusalem Council convened. Peter retold how God gave Gentiles the Holy Spirit without prior conversion to Judaism. James ruled that Gentiles would be accepted into fellowship by keeping the four laws listed above.

The church uses this ruling as proof of freedom from Torah. This misreading avoids verse 21, "For the **Torah** of Moses has been preached in every city from the earliest times and is read in the synagogues on every Sabbath." What really happened?

First, understand that James could not have been saying that Gentiles should be subject to only four laws. That would have allowed blasphemy, coveting, bribery, lying, and murder, to name a few!

Second, what Gentiles miss when reading this passage is why Jews would not want to fellowship with Gentiles in the first place. Gentiles were unclean by contact with the dead, sexual and eating practices, and other ways. Leviticus 5.2-3 says that coming in contact with human uncleanness required sacrifices. Fellowshipping with Gentiles would create the need for constant cleansing rituals. So some Jews wanted the Gentiles to obey all the Torah first. That would be less stressful. But all could see from the testimony of Paul, Barnabas, and Peter that God was accepting Gentiles regardless.

So James ruled that if Gentiles kept just four laws, they could fellowship and *gradually come into compliance with the rest of Torah as they heard Moses preached every Sabbath.* Rather than give a carte blanche for Gentiles to ignore all but four laws, James proposed what the church calls justification followed by sanctification or consecration, the theme of this book. A person is saved by Grace through faith by accepting Yeshua's death as payment for sin. Then a life of obedience begins.

James didn't toss Torah. The Jewish believers were being very gracious toward Gentiles, giving them time to come into compliance, even knowing there would be conflicts.

Didn't Paul Say We're Not under Torah?

Be ready to ask, "Who is Paul, really?"

Look past the ex-Pharisee who allegedly declared Torah nailed to the cross. See Paul who remained a Pharisee, "Men *and* brethren, I am a Pharisee, the son of a Pharisee," Acts 23.6.

See Paul who encouraged his student in 2 Timothy 3.14-17 to continue in the knowledge of the holy Scriptures Timothy learned from youth, *which make one wise to salvation in Yeshua,* are from the mouth of God, and make a man perfect. Paul means Torah and Tenach. He can't mean the New Covenant, because that wasn't completed or canonized yet.

See Paul who refused to circumcise Titus in order to protect justification by faith in Galatians 2.3-5. But don't miss the same Paul who circumcised Timothy in Acts 16.1-3.

See Paul in Acts 21.20-26 who paid for sacrifices for himself and four other men *to prove that he still taught Torah!* Church tradition strains to explain why Paul was offering sacrifices decades after Yeshua's perfect sacrifice.

See Paul who told Governor Felix in Acts 24.14, "But this I confess unto thee, that after the way which they call heresy, so worship I the God of my fathers, believing all things which are written in the **Torah** and in the prophets…"

See Paul's writings, which Peter described in 2 Peter 3.16 as "hard to be understood, which they that are unlearned and unstable wrest, as *they* do also the other scriptures, unto their own destruction." A text removed from its context becomes a pretext. See Paul who loved Torah. Don't "wrest" his letters to teach something else. Now let's take another look at Paul.

Romans 6.14   For sin shall not have dominion over you: for ye are not under the **Torah**, but under grace.

Romans 5 and 6 is about freedom from punishment for breaking Torah. Torah's blessings are good; its curses are deadly. *Yeshua took upon Himself the punishment for breaking Torah—death—and freed us so that we are no longer under the curse of Torah.* The requirement to obey Torah came after salvation. Israel was redeemed by the blood of the lamb at Passover, baptized in the Red Sea, and *then* given Torah at Mt. Sinai. Today, we are redeemed by the blood of the Lamb, baptized, and *then* we begin a life of obedience to Torah. We saw this at the Jerusalem Council: salvation is followed by obedience.

When Israel prepared to enter the Promised Land, Moses warned of Torah's curses for disobedience in Deuteronomy 11.28 and 28.15-68: suffering and death. Hebrews 10.26-31 gives believers a similar warning today.

The next verse, 6.15, says that we should not sin, even though we are no longer under Law. In 1 John 3.4, sin is defined as ἀνομία *anomia* against the Law. Our relief from Torah's death sentence isn't an excuse to break Torah.

If you were arrested for reckless driving, you would have put yourself under the Law. But if the Judge turned out to be your long-lost Dad and He paid the fine for you, *you would be free from the Law.* If He gave you an expense account and a mission, you would have a new life. You would be an ambassador for your Dad. The last thing you would want to be is a scoff-Law! You *could* break the Law, but you *wouldn't want to.* You would keep His Law as perfectly as you could. Even though it wasn't keeping the Law that brought you into your new family, you would know that your Dad keeps the Law in place to guide and protect us.

If Yeshua had fulfilled all traffic law, would you still stop at red lights and stay under the speed limit while driving to church? When you got there, would they call you a legalist? Or is it acceptable to keep man's laws, but not God's?

Aren't We Dead to Torah?

Romans 7.4-6　　　　　　Wherefore, my brethren, ye also are become dead to **Torah** by the body of Christ; that ye should be married to another, *even* to him who is raised from the dead, that we should bring forth fruit unto God. For when we were in the flesh, the motions of sins, which were by **Torah**, did work in our members to bring forth fruit unto death. But now we are delivered from **Torah**, that being dead wherein we were held; that we should serve in newness of spirit, and not in the oldness of the letter.

Believers can't die for breaking Torah now—we already died with Yeshua, then He raised us from the dead! We serve by the Spirit's desire, Romans 4, *not by the threat of the letter.* We establish Torah through faith, Romans 3.31. God forbid that we should sin, Romans 6.1-2. When the church tosses Written Torah, it loses its ability to recognize and avoid sin.

Isn't Christ the End of Torah?

Romans 10.4   For Christ *is* the end of the **Torah** for righteousness to every one that believeth.

Paul was highly educated in Tarsus. Here he used the word τέλος *telos*. Philosophy and Strong's agree on a definition of telos: the end to which all things relate, the aim, purpose. There is a universal perfect chair, the telos of chairs. All furniture makers strive to make that chair. They all fail.

Yeshua is the end to which all Torah relates, its aim, purpose. Torah is the way, Psalm 119.1, the truth, Psalm 119.142, and the life, Deuteronomy 32.46-47. Yeshua is the way, the truth, and the life, John 14.6. In other words, Yeshua is *Torah! Torah! Torah!* We imitate Him, but we fall short. Should furniture makers quit because they can't make the perfect chair? Should we quit seeking Torah because we fall short? Paul says in 1 Corinthians 11.1 that we should follow him as he follows Yeshua. We should keep trying, even if we fail. Do you remember what Yeshua said in Matthew 5.19? It's bad to break Torah. And it's bad to *teach* breaking Torah.

Didn't Paul Do Away with Sabbath?

Romans 14.5-6   One man esteemeth one day above another: another esteemeth every day *alike*. Let every man be fully persuaded in his own mind. He that regardeth the day, regardeth *it* unto the Lord; and he that regardeth not the day, to the Lord he doth not regard *it*. He that eateth, eateth to the Lord, for he giveth God thanks; and he that eateth not, to the Lord he eateth not, and giveth God thanks.

Romans 14 is about food. It never mentions Sabbath. In fact the entire book of Romans never mentions Sabbath. But Sabbath is affirmed repeatedly in Torah. Breaking Sabbath is cause for a death sentence, Numbers 15.32-36. Keeping Sabbath is a בְּרִית עוֹלָם *b'rit olam* perpetual covenant between God and His people, Exodus 31.16. "Perpetual" doesn't stop just because a Roman emperor says it stopped.

In Isaiah 56.1-7 and 58.13-14, God lists blessings for keeping Sabbath. Paul says in 2 Timothy 3.16 that all Scripture (Torah and Tenach) is God-breathed, inspired. Paul isn't putting up for personal opinion what day should be set apart to God.

The last chapter reviewed the Bible's fast days. Believers in Paul's day argued about additional days. An early Christian document called the *Didache,* which some date as early as 40 to 60 AD, says not to fast with the hypocrites on Monday and Thursday, but on Wednesday and Friday. One of the boasts of the Pharisee in Luke 18.12 is that he fasted twice a week. Fasting was a bigger issue in the early church than today.

Paul is saying don't be like the Pharisee in the parable and think you're better than others because you fast certain days.

Didn't the Church Change Sabbath to Sunday?

1 Corinthians 16.2   Upon the first *day* of the week let every one of you lay by him in store, as *God* hath prospered him, that there be no gatherings when I come.

Acts 20.7   And upon the first *day* of the week, when the disciples came together to break bread, Paul preached unto them, ready to depart on the morrow; and continued his speech until midnight.

The Greek word for week is σάββατον *sabbaton* Sabbath, which can also mean the first of the week, as here and in Mark 16.2, the day after Sabbath, what we call Sunday. The word *day* is italicized because it was added by the translators to clarify. Jews don't handle money on Sabbath because Nehemiah strictly enforced not buying and selling on the Sabbath, Nehemiah 13.15-22. So the first day of the week is a better day to handle money. Paul instructed the Gentiles to handle money the way the Jews did. Eisegesis is the error of putting our own presuppositions into a text. Just because *churches today* take a "Sunday morning offering," that doesn't prove that the *early church* changed the Sabbath from the seventh day of the week to the first.

In Acts, the disciples broke bread on the first of the week. When does the week start? For Gentiles, Sunday begins after Saturday midnight.   But the Bible's week begins after Sabbath, which ends on "Saturday night," after sunset, with Havdalah. Havdalah is a buffer between Sabbath and the rest of the week, an occasion for fellowship, prayer, and eating together. That's when Paul and the disciples ate together and Paul preached. Paul didn't start preaching after "Sunday morning service" and go all day into the night. He started after Havdalah, preached late, and left "Sunday morning," a regular work day in Israel then and now.

Didn't Paul Throw Out the Food Laws?

Romans 14.14   I know, and am persuaded by the Lord Jesus, that *there is* nothing unclean of itself: but to him that esteemeth any thing to be unclean, to him *it is* unclean.

1 Corinthians 10.25-28   Whatsoever is sold in the shambles, *that* eat, asking no question for conscience sake: For the earth *is* the Lord's, and the fulness thereof. If any of them that believe not bid you *to a feast*, and ye be disposed to go; whatsoever is set before you, eat, asking no question for conscience sake. But if any man say unto you, This is offered in sacrifice unto idols, eat not for his sake that shewed it, and for conscience sake: for the earth *is* the Lord's, and the fulness thereof:

Galatians 2.11-14   But when Peter was come to Antioch, I withstood him to the face, because he was to be blamed. For before that certain came from James, he did eat with the Gentiles: but when they were come, he withdrew and separated himself, fearing them which were of the circumcision. And the other Jews dissembled likewise with him; insomuch that Barnabas also was carried away with their dissimulation. But when I saw that they walked not uprightly according to the truth of the Gospel, I said unto Peter before *them* all, If thou, being a Jew, livest after the manner of Gentiles, and not as do the Jews, why compellest thou the Gentiles to live as do the Jews?

Romans 14.14 is bad translation. Three times the word κοινός *koinos* common is translated in error as unclean. ἀκάθαρτος *akathartos* unclean is the word *not* used. Common food is clean food which is made common by improper handling or by being offered to an idol. Paul's not addressing Leviticus 11. Pork for example is not clean food and is not addressed here. Leviticus 11.7-8 says don't even touch a swine carcass. Isaiah 66.17 says that those who eat swine's flesh will be destroyed.

Observant Jews avoid food which is either unclean or common. If meat isn't marked kosher, it may contain pork products or blood or it may even have been offered to an idol. Today, halal meat has been offered to the god of the Koran just as kosher meat has been offered to the God of the Bible. Observant Jews take Torah seriously; the church doesn't. That's the difference.

Paul isn't negating Torah, he is telling believers, including Peter, to relax concerning the oral tradition, which still held sway over the circumcision sect. Paul offers a "Don't ask, don't tell" policy. If you don't know the food is common, don't try to find out. If it's been offered to an idol, don't eat it. If you're not sure, and you're worried about it, don't eat it.

It's All about Faith! We Should Ignore Torah!

Galatians 2.16   Knowing that a man is not justified by the works of **Torah**, but by the faith of Jesus Christ, even we have believed in Jesus Christ, that we might be justified by the faith of Christ, and not by the works of **Torah**: for by the works of **Torah** shall no flesh be justified.

This verse was addressed earlier. "Don't you know you can't be justified by the Law?" Yes, we know. There are two ways into God's family: birth or adoption. Doing good works won't help. Salvation is by faith alone. But once in God's family, there are instructions to follow, also known as Torah. And since the very definition of the New Covenant in Jeremiah 31, repeated in Hebrews 8, includes Torah written in the heart, *Torah cannot be done away in the New Covenant!*

Shouldn't We Just Kill the Tutor?

Galatians 3.23-25   But before faith came, we were kept under **Torah**, shut up unto the faith which should afterwards be revealed. Wherefore **Torah** was our schoolmaster *to bring us* unto Christ, that we might be justified by faith. But after that faith is come, we are no longer under a schoolmaster.

Imagine a king who wants his sons to take over the Kingdom. He assigns them a schoolmaster to teach them everything they will need to know in order to govern. When the princes are grown, they have internalized everything the tutor taught them. Should the king then kill the tutor? Of course not! The tutor hasn't become evil simply because the princes internalized their lessons. In the New Covenant, Torah is written in the heart. We should be internalizing Torah, not killing it!

In their series *The Way of the Master*, Ray Comfort and Kirk Cameron employ Torah to witness. They demonstrate that Grace alone doesn't work as a witnessing tool unless and until a person is convicted of sin. Many people assume they're going to heaven because they're "good people." But after being confronted with a few commandments, plus how Yeshua made those commandments even stricter, "You have heard it said…but I tell you…," many hardened hearts eagerly accept God's offer of forgiveness. Ray Comfort's and Kirk Cameron's evangelization method demonstrates that the Tutor's authority is still powerful.

Isn't it Wrong to Keep Jewish Feasts?

Galatians 4.8-11   Howbeit then, when ye knew not God, ye did service unto them which by nature are no gods. But now, after that ye have known God, or rather are known of God, how turn ye again to the weak and beggarly elements, whereunto ye desire again to be in bondage? Ye observe days, and months, and times, and years. I am afraid of you, lest I have bestowed upon you labour in vain.

Note that Paul avoids naming Torah's appointed times, such as Sabbaths, New Moons, or Passover, etc. In Acts 13.51 to 14.23, Paul and Barnabas traveled through *Iconium, Lystra, and Derbe.* In Lystra, they prayed for a lame man who got up and walked. The impact is dramatic, as seen in Acts 14.11-13:

> And when the people saw what Paul had done, they lifted up their voices, saying in the speech of Lycaonia, The gods are come down to us in the likeness of men. And they called Barnabas, Jupiter; and Paul, Mercurius, because he was the chief speaker. Then the priest of Jupiter, which was before their city, brought oxen and garlands unto the gates, and would have done sacrifice with the people.

This map and its accompanying article[1] place the cities of Iconium, Lystra, and Derbe in the province of Galatia:

Galatians were pagans before they accepted Yeshua. Now reread Galatians 4.8-11. What were the "weak and beggarly elements, whereunto ye desire again to be in bondage"? Not Torah's appointed times, *because the Galatians couldn't return to something they never did before.* Paul worried that the Galatians were returning to pagan customs.

Isn't Torah Nailed to the Cross?

Ephesians 2.14-16　　For he is our peace, who hath made both one, and hath broken down the middle wall of partition *between us*; Having abolished in his flesh the enmity, *even* the law of commandments *contained* in ordinances; for to make in himself of twain one new man, *so* making peace; And that he might reconcile both unto God in one body by the cross, having slain the enmity thereby:

Colossians 2.10-17　　And ye are complete in him, which is the head of all principality and power: In whom also ye are circumcised with the circumcision made without hands, in putting off the body of the sins of the flesh by the circumcision of Christ: Buried with him in baptism, wherein also ye are risen with *him* through the faith of the operation of God, who hath raised him from the dead. And you, being dead in your sins and the uncircumcision of your flesh, hath he quickened together with him, having forgiven you all trespasses; Blotting out the handwriting of ordinances that was against us, which was contrary to us, and took it out of the way, nailing it to his cross; *And* having spoiled principalities and powers, he made a shew of them openly, triumphing over them in it.　Let no man therefore judge you in meat, or in drink, or in respect of an holyday, or of the new moon, or of the sabbath *days*: Which are a shadow of things to come; but the body *is* of Christ.

There are several options for the middle wall of partition in Ephesians.[2] 1. A literal wall within the Temple area which separated Jews and Gentiles, with posted warnings to Gentiles that trespassing was a capital offense.　2. The curtain that separated the Most Holy Place from the Holy Place in the Temple.　3. A cosmic boundary which had previously given principalities and powers a mediating position between God and man through law.　4. "The fence around the law" created by the rabbis, whose multitude of legal interpretations, applications, and additions protected Torah but also separated Jew and Gentile.

A fence around a command can be a good thing. There is no command against a male pastor counseling a female. But if he does so privately over a period of time, it can lead to disaster. A certain pastor put a fence around adultery. He installed a large window between his office and other staff so that they could watch, but not hear, his counseling sessions.

But fences can also block obedience to commands. Yeshua rebuked the Pharisees for this in Mark 7.6-13 and Matthew 15.1-20, and again in Matthew 23. God told the prophet Ezekiel how Israel had rebelled even in the wilderness, so He gave them consequences, Ezekiel 20.24-25, "Because they had not executed my judgments, but had despised my statutes, and had polluted my sabbaths, and their eyes were after their fathers' idols. Wherefore I gave them also statutes *that were* not good, and judgments whereby they should not live…" God allowed Israel, once they rejected Torah, to fall under statutes and traditions that bring death!

Living Torah was nailed to the cross. Was Written Torah also? Let's say yes. We still have Yeshua's guarantee in Matthew 5.17-19 that Torah is still very much alive. So it seems that the only part of Written Torah that stayed dead was its curse. Or the later commandments and ordinances that were against Israel were nailed to the cross.

Not familiar with harmful commands of oral law, the church assumes that Written Torah was nailed to the cross. Recognizing the havoc that would result from canceling all of Torah, the church keeps some, the Nine Commandments for example. The church creates an artificial separation between "moral Law" and "ceremonial Law." For example: "Since Mt 5:17 and Ro 3:31 teach that God's moral standard expressed in the OT law is not changed by the coming of Christ, what is abolished here is probably the effect of the specific 'commandments and regulations' in separating Jews from Gentiles, whose nonobservance of the Jewish law renders them ritually unclean."[3] But Written Torah already allowed Gentiles to join Israel. It was Torah's curse and the manmade commandments and ordinances which died at the cross.

Before Yeshua, Jew and Gentile shared a predicament. Torah's curse and ordinances of men kept both away from God. Yeshua smashed that glass ceiling. He broke through from heaven to earth to tabernacle with us. He condemned false teaching. He nailed Torah's curse to His cross. They died together, but only One rose. We join Israel through God's Lamb Who adopts us into His family. We begin fellowship with four commands. We'll get the rest in time.

It's worthwhile to do a Strong's search in the King James Version on the word "death." In Torah you'll see "shall be put to death" many times. Death is a frequent answer for Torah violations. But in the letters of the New Covenant, a word search on "death" reveals a much different answer. Yeshua "by his death" *frees us from the death we earned* by breaking Torah. Now we can seek Torah's blessings without its death penalty hanging over our heads.

Paul also contrasted human philosophy, the context of Colossians 2, with Torah commands in verses 16-17: appointed times, New Moons, and Sabbath. Like the Galatians, the Colossians faced ridicule from friends and relatives who had not accepted Yeshua. But unlike the Galatians, the Colossians stayed faithful to Torah. Paul encouraged them not to be judged for keeping Torah, which is superior to human tradition. Isaiah 66.23 tells of the last days, "And it shall come to pass, *that* from one new moon to another, and from one sabbath to another, shall all flesh come to worship before me, saith the LORD." Paul wasn't rebuking the Colossians for keeping Torah's appointed days.

Torah's appointed times are a shadow; the reality is Yeshua. The spring feasts remind us that Yeshua paid Torah's death penalty as God's Passover Lamb. He was wrapped in linen and buried for Unleavened Bread, and He rose from the dead on First Fruits. Yeshua sent the Holy Spirit on Shavuot. The fall feasts remind us that Yeshua will be crowned King on Trumpets. Yom Kippur brings judgment. Tabernacles marks the beginning of the age of Yeshua dwelling on earth with us. These shadows are reason to watch and celebrate!

Doesn't the Spirit Cancel Torah?

1 Timothy 4.1-5 Now the Spirit speaketh expressly, that in the latter times some shall depart from the faith, giving heed to seducing spirits, and doctrines of devils; Speaking lies in hypocrisy; having their conscience seared with a hot iron; Forbidding to marry, *and commanding* to abstain from meats, which God hath created to be received with thanksgiving of them which believe and know the truth. For every creature of God *is* good, and nothing to be refused, if it be received with thanksgiving: For it is sanctified by the word of God and prayer.

As in Colossians 2, Paul distinguishes between Torah and vain philosophies. God's Torah is perfect; man's traditions aren't.

In Paul's day, Gnosticism, from the Greek meaning learned, was similar to today's New Age movement. Gnostics believed that they could transcend the lower, imperfect, or evil world of matter to the spiritual god-world of perfection. Curiously, Gnostics believed in Yeshua's deity, which they considered good, but not His physical body, which they considered evil. Various ascetic disciplines accomplished this alleged transcendence. Sexual abstinence was one such discipline. But Torah advocates marriage, even for priests. And the Bible is full of thanks to God for various blessings and pleasures. Paul referred to Gnosticism or another philosophy, not Torah.

It's wrong to refuse that which God created to be received with thanksgiving by them who know the truth. Torah is truth, and we know what it says. Leviticus 11 defines certain animals as unclean. Did God change His mind? Where does God say that we can now receive what is unclean with thanks? Even after Yeshua, Peter refused to eat unclean animals. Marriage is good and has limits; eating is good and has limits. Paul's not canceling Leviticus 11.

So often we hear in the church, "I prayed about it and God told me it's OK to..." We see sin easily excused as if Paul never wrote Romans or Corinthians. We'll find our way through this moral fog by keeping our eyes on the Instruments.

Doesn't Hebrews Outlaw Sabbath and Feasts?

Hebrews 4.4-11   For he spake in a certain place of the seventh *day* on this wise, And God did rest the seventh day from all his works. And in this *place* again, If they shall enter into my rest. Seeing therefore it remaineth that some must enter therein, and they to whom it was first preached entered not in because of unbelief: Again, he limiteth a certain day, saying in David, To day, after so long a time; as it is said, To day if ye will hear his voice, harden not your hearts. For if Jesus had given them rest, then would he not afterward have spoken of another day. There remaineth therefore a rest to the people of God. For he that is entered into his rest, he also hath ceased from his own works, as God *did* from his. Let us labour therefore to enter into that rest, lest any man fall after the same example of unbelief.

Hebrews 10.1, 26-29   For the law having a shadow of good things to come, *and* not the very image of the things, can never with those sacrifices which they offered year by year continually make the comers thereunto perfect… For if we sin wilfully after that we have received the knowledge of the truth, there remaineth no more sacrifice for sins, But a certain fearful looking for of judgment and fiery indignation, which shall devour the adversaries. He that despised Moses' law died without mercy under two or three witnesses: Of how much sorer punishment, suppose ye, shall he be thought worthy, who hath trodden under foot the Son of God, and hath counted the blood of the covenant, wherewith he was sanctified, an unholy thing, and hath done despite unto the Spirit of grace?

Read Hebrews 3 and 4 with Psalm 95, a Sabbath psalm which they quote. And all of Hebrews 10.

Some argue that Hebrews 4 cancels Sabbath observance and Hebrews 10 cancels observance of any "shadow" such as the feasts. Hank Hanegraaff, the Bible Answer Man and noted Bible expert, responded with Hebrews 10 when a listener asked why the church doesn't keep Passover:

> To go back to a type and a shadow when the substance has come makes no sense. It makes no more sense than going back to Temple priest and sacrifice when the ultimate sacrificial Lamb has come. Again, the writer of Hebrews speaks to this question in no uncertain terms. To go back to the shadow when the substance has come is like trampling underfoot the sacred blood of Jesus Christ. I think that's the point that's paramount in the discussion.[4]

Exodus 12.14 says to keep Passover forever. Mr. Hanegraaff says that keeping Passover is trampling the blood of Christ. So we have a simple, ancient choice: Bible or tradition.

Luke 22.19 records Yeshua's words, "And he took bread, and gave thanks, and brake *it*, and gave unto them, saying, This is my body which is given for you: this do in remembrance of me." Yeshua commanded us to keep Passover. Tradition changed this command to the practice of the Eucharist or communion. Paul said to keep Passover and Unleavened Bread in 1 Corinthians 5.7-8, "Purge out therefore the old leaven, that ye may be a new lump, as ye are unleavened. For even Christ our passover is sacrificed for us: Therefore let us keep the feast, not with old leaven, neither with the leaven of malice and wickedness; but with the unleavened *bread* of sincerity and truth." Paul's encouragement is like Hebrews': purge sin.

Hebrews 10 compares shadows to Yeshua's perfect sacrifice. Then it reaffirms that the New Covenant is Torah in our heart (including Passover!) and forgiveness. With sin forgiven, there is no more need for sacrifices. This wonderfully new, bold life of Grace and faith in Yeshua is contrasted with returning to sin and its devastating consequences. What could be worse than escaping judgment by a gift of Grace only to fall again into the judgment of God? Once saved, or at least once tasting Grace, we are literally playing with fire to turn our backs on that Grace. But to conclude from Hebrews that keeping Passover is like trampling underfoot the sacred blood of Jesus Christ, that's outrageous.

Israel kept Passover for centuries. Only by faith could they know that they were also keeping a shadow of the sacrifice of God's perfect Lamb, Who would one day grant freedom from sin. Did Israel sin by remembering redemption in Egypt? In Matthew 26.27-29, 39, Yeshua instituted the New Covenant, even knowing that He would suffer terribly to accomplish it. He promised to celebrate anew with us in the Kingdom of Heaven. How is it a sin to remember this redemption?

If keeping Passover "makes no more sense than going back to Temple priest and sacrifice when the ultimate sacrificial Lamb has come," why did Paul offer sacrifices in Acts 21.20-26? After Yeshua returns and His kingdom is reestablished in Jerusalem, why do the priests in Ezekiel 45.21 keep Passover?

If it's so bad to celebrate shadows after the reality has come, do Christians trample the blood of Christ when celebrating the shadow of Easter? Why is it acceptable to celebrate feasts with pagan origins, but not the Bible's appointed times? Some get the mistaken impression from Hebrews 10.1 and Colossians 2.17 that shadows are bad. But shadows prove reality. Your shadow proves you. Yeshua's shadows prove Him. Yeshua's shadows point us to His reality.

When faced with challenges like this in our Torah journey, it's helpful to check our waypoints. Some of these waypoints are listed on page 147. Torah is to be written in our heart. When that truth was lost, the church turned away from God's basic instructions to commandments of men.

The original Bible Answer Man, Walter Martin, addressed an error based on John 10.10 that God never causes stealing, killing, or destruction. Some people say that since Satan does only those three things, God cannot do them at all. Walter Martin called that conclusion a non-sequitur, lightheartedly defined as, "It don't follow no how, Baby."

Passover is a memorial and shadow of what God did in Egypt and what Yeshua did on the cross. If anyone says that keeping Passover has become a sin, that don't follow no how, Baby.

Some argue that Hebrews 4 is an argument against Sabbath. Since Yeshua is our Sabbath rest, they say, it's now a sin to keep the weekly Sabbath.

The KJV mistranslates Hebrews 4.9, "There remaineth therefore a rest to the people of God." Rest is σαββατισμός *sabbatismos* a keeping Sabbath, the blessed rest from toils and troubles looked for in the age to come. Hebrews 4 does emphasize an eternal Sabbath rest for true believers in Yeshua, a rest which begins now if we prove our faith with action. That's why verse 11 says that we must "labour therefore to enter into that rest." But Hebrews 4 doesn't cancel the seventh-day Sabbath, the Fourth Commandment, any more than Hebrews 10 cancels the appointed times.

We can avoid much confusion by keeping the bright line in mind: on one side of the line, we are saved by Grace through faith in the sacrificial death of Yeshua. On the other side, after salvation, we have a lot of work to do. Written Torah tells us what that work is. Living Torah showed us how to do it.

Isn't Torah Just an Old Wineskin?

Matthew 9.16-17   No man putteth a piece of new cloth unto an old garment, for that which is put in to fill it up taketh from the garment, and the rent is made worse. Neither do men put new wine into old bottles: else the bottles break, and the wine runneth out, and the bottles perish: but they put new wine into new bottles, and both are preserved.

Bottles is the KJV word for wineskins. Did Yeshua say that, just as a new patch will tear an old garment or new wine will burst an old wineskin, He brought a new teaching and Torah is done away with? Is there now a "change of dispensation" and Law is replaced with Grace? Is this an explanation of John 1.17, "For the law was given by Moses, *but* grace and truth came by Jesus Christ"? Was this Yeshua's announcement that Judaism had served its purpose and He was beginning a new Gentile church?

As noted earlier, most think that Yeshua created *ecclesia* the church. But ecclesia is the Septuagint's word for the assembly of Israel. And Stephen used it in Acts 7.38 to mean Israel in the wilderness. Yeshua didn't create a church to replace Israel and Torah.

Look at Matthew 9, Mark 2, and Luke 5. These all follow a similar outline: Yeshua tells a paralytic that his sin is forgiven. The Pharisees accuse Yeshua of blasphemy. Yeshua proves His authority to forgive sin by healing the man. Yeshua selects Matthew as a disciple and soon eats with tax collectors and sinners. The Pharisees are upset that Yeshua feasts with sinners instead of fasting with the righteous like they do. Yeshua responds each time with patches and wineskins.

The old wineskins were the experts with too many religious preconceptions to accept Yeshua as God's promised Messiah. This is the same fault Yeshua exposed in Matthew 21.32. Tax collectors and prostitutes welcomed John's message and repented, but Pharisees couldn't. The disciples who changed the world were young at heart. They were open to Yeshua's forgiveness of sin and God's imminent Kingdom.

Old wineskins are the experts who are certain that Torah and Israel are passé. They're even more certain if their salary depends on it. It's possible for them to let go of traditions and make room for some new wine. But new wineskins are ready and waiting to get packed full of Written and Living Torah.

Old
wineskin
or new:
which
are you?

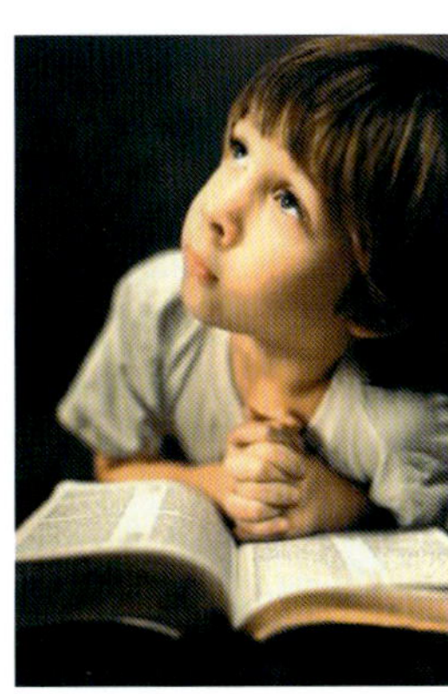

Flight Lessons

Yeshua broke the glass ceiling and granted us clearance for the Kingdom of Heaven. This helps us understand Paul when he contrasts "life in the Spirit" vs. "the dead letter of the Law."

Taking Off   Two of my sons are commercial pilots. I've been impressed with the amount of training required to lift a complicated piece of metal into the sky and keep it there. A pilot-in-training first learns principles of flight which include thrust and drag, lift and gravity. The engine provides thrust to overcome drag. The wings provide lift to overcome gravity. Gravity requires the pilot to maintain lift. Drag requires the pilot to maintain thrust. In every moment of flight the pilot is occupied with monitoring lift and thrust to maintain safe flight. A pilot who thought he or she could take off without another care would probably just become a warning to other pilots.

Trusting the Instruments   An instrument rating allows a pilot to fly in zero visibility, so it's a necessary certification for commercial pilots. The training forces the pilot to overcome vertigo and distractions. A hood is placed over the pilot's eyes to block the windshield and show only the instruments. One of my sons described his instrument check ride. During a blind landing approach, gusts bucked his plane up and down and side to side, his radio skipped frequencies, and his examiner peppered him with random questions. Such training forces the pilot in darkness or fog to trust the instruments above all. Otherwise, a pilot could experience vertigo and, though flying straight and level, be sure that the plane is banking or climbing. If the pilot ignores the instruments and counters a nonexistent bank or climb, the result could be disaster. Even veteran commercial pilots may warn their copilots, "Watch me, I've got the leans." It's necessary to trust the instruments to be a successful pilot.

Breaking the Chain   It's usually not one mistake, but a series of mistakes that results in a crash. So the industry stresses the importance of "breaking the chain." Correcting just one error can break the chain and prevent disaster.

Cruising in the Spirit　　Living Torah always set His course through the Control Tower and He always followed Written Torah. Yeshua showed us how to soar. Stress is part of this training process and forces us to focus on the Instruments. The goal is safe flight to accomplish our mission. The warnings delivered throughout Scripture are encouragements to break the chain of pilot error.

Salvation in Yeshua transforms a body of sin into a new life held aloft by רוּחַ *ruach* wind and Spirit. Wind creates lift to counter gravity and death. Spirit creates thrust to counter drag and sin. But gravity and drag do not cease to exist. Neither do death and sin cease to exist. If we stall at just believing and never get our Instrument rating, if we set our own course or try to stay aloft on our own power, death and sin come back in full force. We would just become a warning to other believers. So through prayer we get our mission from the Control Tower. When disoriented by storms, darkness, or fog, we keep our eyes on Written and Living Torah to avoid course deviation. We may need to warn a friend, "Watch me, I've got the leans." The friend can contact the Tower for us and encourage us to watch the Instruments. This is how we break the chain of pilot error. Then we can explore the Kingdom of Heaven, endure storms, and teach others to fly.

As we rack up flight hours and internalize the Tutor, we will begin to receive signals directly from the Spirit. And in-flight perks will become the norm—"love, joy, peace, longsuffering, gentleness, goodness, faith, meekness, and temperance." But since we are always subject to pilot error, distractions, and vertigo, we still need to verify with the Instruments.

Our old nature died with Yeshua and we live anew with Him when wind rushes over our wings. Life in the Spirit doesn't cancel out sin and death. But the forgiveness and life we find in Yeshua's death and resurrection allow us to soar as He did: a course set by the Control Tower, a life according to Torah.

The traditional objections to Torah fade into the distance.

The experts are wrong.

Chapter 4
Where Do We Go from Here?

The Journey

On our annual trip, my son Nathanael and I tried to hike into the Alpine Lakes Wilderness without preparation. As we climbed higher and the snow got deeper, we saw the danger and turned around. Other years we ran into different snags. Finally we were fully prepared with topo maps, waypoints on our GPS, and all the gear. Then we hit a deer as it sprinted across I-90. After spending the night in a tow yard, I called Susan the next morning and she encouraged us to rent a car. I prayed to hitch a ride. William, a friend who lived 100 miles away, saw me while out riding his motorcycle and gave me a chilly ride to a distant car rental. Nathanael and I completed our journey.

That's how it is seeking Torah. We've heard that Torah is for today. We explore, but soon realize that there are hazards we didn't anticipate. We have to reassess. We study. We establish waypoints. When we're ready, something could threaten to derail the whole adventure. We have to ask ourselves why we're doing this. Is it important enough to keep going? We're tempted to give up. We step out in prayer and—surprise! Like William showing up on his motorcycle, suddenly we see a way to keep going.

Waypoints

Has your enthusiasm waned as your Torah journey has been stalled by hazards or objections? Set some waypoints:

- Torah will outlast heaven and earth.
- Yeshua showed us how to keep Torah.
- God promised curses for breaking Torah.
- God promised blessings for keeping Torah.
- Torah is obedience, not a means to salvation.
- Traditions are OK until they contradict Torah.
- God wants us to have Torah written in our heart.

People will challenge us, "Why won't you eat pork? Are you Jewish now? Don't you know Jesus declared all foods clean? Are you trying to earn righteousness through the Law? Don't you know you can lose your salvation doing that?" With our waypoints, we can navigate around these hazards.

If friends or family raise the cost of seeking Written and Living Torah, will we keep going like the Colossians? Or will we return to pagan traditions like the Galatians? Once when I was at an intersection of faith and danger, my friend Don challenged me, "You just have to decide whether you're going to live your life by the Word of God or not." Are we going to follow what the Bible says or will we stick with the safety and comfort of tradition? If we're honestly seeking Written and Living Torah, God will show the way.

Adventure

Seekers past and present, Jew and Gentile, bring treasures out of their storehouses. As an example, consider that Joseph was *thirty* when he stood before Pharaoh and *"began his ministry."* When his *brothers* arrived, they thought he was a *Gentile.*   Since they had planned to *kill him* and thought he was now *dead*, Joseph *hid his identity* from his brothers until he was sure *their hearts had changed.* When *Judah offered himself as a ransom* to save their *father* from the loss of another *faithful son*, Joseph burst into tears and *revealed himself to them.* See any parallels to Yeshua? In Judaism, one of the names for Messiah is *Son of Joseph.* Once you find Torah treasure, you may never want to stop digging!

Many Jews don't want to hear about Yeshua. That's mainly because of church traditions which slandered Written and Living Torah. But some Jewish traditions are also at fault. Yeshua always criticized *any* tradition which contradicted Torah. So we need to guard against trading unbiblical church traditions for unbiblical Jewish traditions. Then we can gain from the vast storehouse of Jewish wisdom without converting to commandments of men. That still leaves a variety of flight plans to express our faith.

The western church was blissfully ignorant of Islamism before 9-11. We thought that freedom from slavery, rights, and tolerance were the result of social evolution. 9-11 was a tear in that fantasy. Now we see how governments based on the Koran are so violent toward women, Jews, Christians, and freedom. We hadn't evolved. We were protected by systems built on the Bible. And now those systems are crumbling. Our culture is hostile to biblical faith but insists that Islam is peaceful. Marriage is redefined and fornication is accepted. Children are sacrificed for prosperity and we don't see the idolatry. Salaries for priests and pastors depend on putting tradition over Torah. God's judgment is inevitable. Unless as believers we are courageous enough to humble ourselves, pray, seek God's face, and turn from our evil ways.

When we understand that God's perfect Torah is eternal, that Yeshua and all the Bible's authors confirmed that, then we can stop being editors of God's Word. We can begin to undo the damage begun by Torah's first editor when he promised, "Ye shall not surely die."

Jews and Gentiles find common ground in Written Torah. When Yeshua returns, we will find common ground in Living Torah. What an awesome time this is to be alive! Ancient prophecies are unfolding and we get to be part of it. Will you return to the Instruments and the church's original course?

More challenge and treasure await those who plunge into Hebrew. The next page lists resources for those who crave learning. It's been said that you can write poetry only in your native language. But perhaps there are some reading this who will become poetic in their new language, Hebrew.

And some could fulfill Micah and Isaiah, saying,

> And many nations shall come, and say, Come, and let us go up to the mountain of the LORD, and to the house of the God of Jacob; and he will teach us of his ways, and we will walk in his paths: for the **Torah** shall go forth of Zion, and the word of the LORD from Jerusalem.

Hebrew Resources

Free

www.torahinmyheart.com Click on Read the Bible in Hebrew for an alef-bet chart and how to get started.

www.blueletterbible.org Click Tools to see the Hebrew text and root words. Click the root word for Strong's.

www.mechon-mamre.org Click Parallel Hebrew and English to see them side by side. Once you've selected a chapter, click Listen to this Chapter in Hebrew.

www.torahportions.org Weekly Torah schedule.

www.in-hebrew.co.il Over 1,200 phrases with audio.

www.israel365.com Hebrew verses emailed every day.

www.hebrew4christians.com Tons of information.

www.translate.google.com Especially useful when you learn to input Hebrew with your keyboard and camera.

Not So Free

www.hebrewworld.com Dr. Danny Ben Gigi's site. The *Hebrew-English Phonetic Bible* has each verse of Tenach with Hebrew, transliteration, and translation. *This is the best resource of all.* You get confidence in pronunciation. His new *Biblical Hebrew Home Study* is also great for the beginners. Dr. Ben Gigi is a native Hebrew speaker and taught biblical Hebrew at Arizona State University for fifteen years.

www.olivetree.com Downloadable Bible versions (such as NKJV with Strong's) for your desktop computer, tablet, or smart phone. Olive Tree also has a BHS morphology app, which examines the grammar for each word of the Tenach.

Hebrew Bible by Zev Clementson. My favorite Apple app for reading Tenach in Hebrew. Side-by-side Hebrew and English or just Hebrew. Strong's too. Same Hebrew audio as the mechon-mamre site.

www.pimsleur.com Best for modern conversational Hebrew. Ads claim that you will learn in half an hour a day. No. Instead, think of training for a marathon, two hours a day.

A Reader's Hebrew Bible by A. Philip Brown. If you want to unplug, this book version of Tenach is for you. It has every Hebrew word used less often than 100 times defined at the bottom of each page, plus a glossary in back.

The *Hebrew-English Phonetic Bible* allows you to begin reading Hebrew right away. Since this Bible loads onto your computer, you can make the pages larger for easier reading. Page reprinted with permission from Hebrew World Inc.

Verse 16 contains the words דָּרֹשׁ דָּרַשׁ *da-rosh da-rash* seek, seek. The middle two words of Torah show Moses diligently seeking the goat of the sin offering for the congregation of Israel.

Leviticus 10

טז. וְאֵת שְׂעִיר הַחַטָּאת דָּרֹשׁ דָּרַשׁ מֹשֶׁה וְהִנֵּה שֹׂרָף וַיִּקְצֹף עַל-אֶלְעָזָר וְעַל-אִיתָמָר בְּנֵי אַהֲרֹן הַנּוֹתָרִם לֵאמֹר:

16. Ve•et se•eer ha•cha•tat da•rosh da•rash Mo•shé ve•hi•né soraf va•yik•tzof al -El•a•zar ve•al-Eeta•mar b'néy Aha•rón ha•no•ta•rim le•mor.

16. And Moses diligently sought the goat of the sin offering, and, behold, it was burned; and he was angry with Eleazar and Ithamar, the sons of Aaron, who were left alive, saying,

---

יז. מַדּוּעַ לֹא-אֲכַלְתֶּם אֶת-הַחַטָּאת בִּמְקוֹם הַקֹּדֶשׁ כִּי קֹדֶשׁ קָדָשִׁים הִוא וְאֹתָהּ נָתַן לָכֶם לָשֵׂאת אֶת-עֲוֹן הָעֵדָה לְכַפֵּר עֲלֵיהֶם לִפְנֵי יְהֹוָה:

17. Ma•dú•a lo-a•chal•tem et-ha•cha•tat bim•kom ha•kó•desh ki Kó•desh Ko•da•shim hee ve•ota na•tan la•chém la•set et-avon ha•eda le•cha•per a•ley•hém lif•néy Adonái.

17. Why have you not eaten the sin offering in the holy place, seeing it is Most Holy, and God has given it to you to bear the iniquity of the congregation, to make atonement for them before the Lord?

יח. הֵן לֹא-הוּבָא אֶת-דָּמָהּ אֶל-הַקֹּדֶשׁ פְּנִימָה אָכוֹל תֹּאכְלוּ אֹתָהּ בַּקֹּדֶשׁ כַּאֲשֶׁר צִוֵּיתִי:

18. Hen lo-hu•va et-da•máh el-ha•kó•desh pe•ní•ma achol toch•lu o•táh ba•kó•desh ka•a•shér tzi•véy•ti.

18. Behold, its blood was not brought inside the holy place; you should indeed have eaten it in the holy place, as I commanded.

יט. וַיְדַבֵּר אַהֲרֹן אֶל-מֹשֶׁה הֵן הַיּוֹם הִקְרִיבוּ אֶת-חַטָּאתָם וְאֶת-עֹלָתָם לִפְנֵי יְהֹוָה וַתִּקְרֶאנָה אֹתִי כָּאֵלֶּה וְאָכַלְתִּי חַטָּאת הַיּוֹם הַיִּיטַב בְּעֵינֵי יְהֹוָה:

19. Va•ye•da•ber Aha•rón el-Mo•shé hen ha•yom hik•rí•vu et-cha•ta•tam ve•et-o•la•tam lif•néy Adonái va•tik•ré•na o•ti ka•é•le ve•a•chál•ti cha•tat ha•yom ha•yi•tav be•ey•néy Adonái.

19. And Aaron said to Moses, Behold, this day have they offered their sin offering and their burnt offering before the Lord; and such things have befallen me; and if I had eaten the sin offering to day, should it have been accepted in the sight of the Lord?

כ. וַיִּשְׁמַע מֹשֶׁה וַיִּיטַב בְּעֵינָיו:

20. Va•yish•ma Mo•shé va•yi•tav be•ey•nav.

20. And when Moses heard that, he was content.

Chapter 5
Loving Each Other

Name-Calling "Legalist!" and "Backslider!" are two words that are best avoided.

First, "Legalist!" may be used by those who think that the Torah has been abolished to describe a Torah seeker. They think that Torah seekers are trying to gain salvation through works of the Law.

Second, "Legalist!" could refer to one using the letter of the Law or a tradition to avoid the intent of Torah. Recall Yeshua scolding the Pharisees for this, such as Matthew 23. An example could be one who, since he isn't a judge, thinks that the prohibition against bribes in Deuteronomy 16.18-19 doesn't apply to him. But how would you feel if a doctor accepted a bribe to treat a less serious case before he got to you? Ignoring a command for pride or gain could be legalism.

Third, "Legalist!" or "Backslider!" may be used by Torah seekers to judge another's heart attitude, as the Pharisee did in scorning the "sinner" in Luke 18.9-14. Yeshua told this parable "…unto certain which trusted in themselves that they were righteous, and despised others…"

A story in Judaism relates to Yeshua's parable. A man dreamed of a ladder of righteousness with people at various rungs. Upset at who seemed lower or higher, specifically a rabbi who was lower, the man reported his dream to his rabbi. The rabbi said that, without knowing one's direction, up or down, there's not enough information to interpret the dream.

We may think we know another's status, but direction and struggle are not easy to determine. We haven't "walked a mile in his moccasins." Charges of "Legalist!" and "Backslider!" tend to generate heat and no light, yet many think that they are justified in using these labels. See the chart on the following page for how easy it is to misuse these terms.

Observance	Name-Calling
Yeshua followed Torah perfectly.	Of course, no one wants to call Yeshua, "Legalist!"
A more-observant person.	"Legalist!" "Pharisee!" "Hypocrite!"
A believer may see himself or herself as "just right" and engage in name-calling.	"I'm OK, you're not."
A less-observant person.	"Backslider!" "Tax collector!" "Pagan!"

Yeshua didn't call someone a hypocrite unless the person only pretended to seek Torah. Or if the person put tradition over Torah. And He said that tax collectors and sinners were entering the Kingdom of Heaven ahead of "the righteous." Imitate Yeshua by dropping careless name-calling.

John 4 shows how Yeshua treated a Samaritan woman. He didn't humiliate or disrespect her. Like a shepherd He cared, taught, corrected, healed, comforted, and redeemed her.

Micah 6.8 is another guide. "He hath shewed thee, O man, what *is* good; and what doth the LORD require of thee, but to do justly, and to love mercy, and to walk humbly with thy God?" We should be just, merciful, and humble. Many are pursuing God the best they can. None of us who is still on earth has entered into full wisdom and obedience in God's Kingdom.

The Evil Tongue   We know that slander is bad, but what if the rumor is true? The term for unnecessary true speech in Judaism is לְשׁוֹן הָרַע *lashon hara* the evil tongue. Four general requirements for speech to be lashon hara are that it is 1) True 2) Negative 3) Not generally known and 4) Serving no emergency purpose. I can think of many times I wish I had known these rules and kept my mouth shut in order to keep another person's dignity intact. Words are like arrows: we only control them until they leave our mouths.

Mocking   Psalms opens with, "Blessed *is* the man…that sitteth [not] in the seat of the scornful." Scorn or mocking is putting another down to make ourselves look better. By mocking Jews, the church assisted its own blindness to Torah. Torah seekers don't appreciate hearing, "Do you kill someone for working on Sabbath?" Neither should we mock.

We are all at different stages. Some jump at every chance to follow Torah in all aspects of life—that doesn't make them legalists. Some hold on to bad habits and comforting traditions longer than others—that doesn't make them backsliders. If we remember that we are no one's Holy Spirit, we'll find it easier to get along.

Confronting When Necessary

Yeshua promised that there will be weeds in the wheat and wolves in sheep's clothing. He warned us to be as wise as serpents and as innocent as doves. We must be on guard— even among "Torah teachers." As Mark Biltz says, listening is like eating chicken: enjoy the meat and spit out the bones.

Yeshua gave instruction in Matthew 18.15-17 [1] on how to confront when necessary. We practiced a modified version of this when our children were little as a way to stop tattling. Now as adults they love and respect each other. Life involves conflict. It's better to deal with conflict rather than pretend that it doesn't exist. Unresolved conflict creates division. "Open rebuke *is* better than secret love," Proverbs 27.5. If we really care about others, we will confront in love. Man up. Yeshua explained how to confront when we must.

Ma Tovoo

מַה טֹּבוּ אֹהָלֶיךָ יַעֲקֹב, מִשְׁכְּנֹתֶיךָ יִשְׂרָאֵל.
Yis-ra-el mish-ke-no-te-cha Ya-a-kov oh-ha-le-cha to-voo Ma
oh Israel. your dwelling places oh Jacob, are your tents goodly How

Numbers 24.5

וַאֲנִי, בְּרֹב חַסְדְּךָ, אָבֹא בֵיתֶךָ.
vey-te-cha a-vo chas-de-cha be-rov Va-ani,
to Your house. will come with Your great mercy, And I,

אֶשְׁתַּחֲוֶה אֶל הֵיכַל קָדְשְׁךָ בְּיִרְאָתֶךָ.
be-yir-a-te-cha kod-she-cha hey-chal el Esh-ta-cha-ve
with deep respect. of Your holiness the temple before I will bow

Psalm 5.8

יְיָ, אָהַבְתִּי מְעוֹן בֵּיתֶךָ,
bey-te-cha, me-on a-hav-ti Adonai
Your house, I love HASHEM

וּמְקוֹם מִשְׁכַּן כְּבוֹדֶךָ.
ke-vo-de-cha mish-kan oo-me-kom
Your honor. of dwelling and the place

Psalm 26.8

וַאֲנִי אֶשְׁתַּחֲוֶה וְאֶכְרָעָה,
ve-ech-ra-ah, esh-ta-cha-ve Va-a-ni
and kneel, shall bow And I

אֶבְרְכָה לִפְנֵי יְיָ עֹשִׂי.
o-si Adonai lif-ney ev-re-cha
my Creator. HASHEM before I shall praise

Psalm 95.6

וַאֲנִי תְפִלָּתִי לְךָ יְיָ, עֵת רָצוֹן,
ra-tzon et Adonai, le-cha te-fi-la-ti Va-a-ni
of acceptance, at this time HASHEM, to You pledge my prayer And I

אֱלֹהִים, בְּרָב־חַסְדֶּךָ, עֲנֵנִי בֶּאֱמֶת יִשְׁעֶךָ.
yish-e-cha be-e-met a-ne-ni chas-de-cha, be-rov Elohim,
with Your true salvation. answer me with Your great mercy, HASHEM,

Psalm 69.13

Appendix
Hebrew Prayer

A Prayer to Our Father

(Hebrew reads from right to left.)

אָבִינוּ שֶׁבַּשָּׁמַיִם יִתְקַדֵּשׁ שְׁמְךָ
avee-noo she-ba-sha-mai-yeem yeet-ka-desh sheem-cha
Our Father in heaven may it be sanctified Your Name.

וְיִתְבָּרֵךְ מַלְכוּתְךָ רְצוֹנְךָ יִהְיֶה עָשׂוּי
ve-yeet-ba-rech mal-choot-cha re-tson-cha yee-h'-ye a-sui
may it be blessed Your Kingdom. Your will shall be done

בַּשָּׁמַיִם וּבָאָרֶץ וְתִתֶּן לַחְמֵנוּ תְּמִידִית
ba-sh-mai-yeem oo-va-a-rets ve-tee-ten lach-me-noo te-mee-deet
in heaven and on earth. And give our bread daily.

וּמְחוֹל לָנוּ חַטֹאתֵינוּ
oo-me-chol la-noo cha-to-tay-noo
And forgive the debt to us of our sins

כַּאֲשֶׁר אֲנַחְנוּ מוֹחֲלִים לַחוֹטְאִים לָנוּ
ka-a-sher a-nach-noo mo-cha-leem la-chot-teem la-noo
as we forgive the debt of those who sin against us.

וְאַל תְּבִיאֵנוּ לִידֵי נִסָּיוֹן
ve-al te-vee-ay-noo lee-day nees-sa-yon
And do not bring us into the hands of a test.

וְשָׁמְרֵנוּ מִכָּל רָע. אָמֵן
ve-shom-ray-noo mee-kol rah a-men
And protect us from all evil. Amen.

Reprinted with permission.
To hear *A Prayer to Our Father* recited in Hebrew,
go to www.aprayertoourfather.com and click on
Media/Audio/Learn the Prayer in Hebrew.

Endnotes

Introduction

1.   John 1.1, 14, "In the beginning was the Word, and the Word was with God, and the Word was God…And the Word was made flesh, and dwelt among us, (and we beheld his glory, the glory as of the only begotten of the Father,) full of grace and truth."

2.   *Thayer's Greek Lexicon: Diotrephes* is "nourished by Zeus or Foster Child of Zeus…a Christian man, but proud and arrogant." In 3 John 9, ἀδελφός *adelphos* brethren, of the same womb describes whom Diotrephes kicked out of the church. Thayer's for G80, definition #2, allows for adelphos to be the equivalent of the Hebrew אָח *ach* brother, having the same national ancestry, belonging to the same people, countryman, meaning fellow Jew. Examples where the Septuagint translates אָח as ἀδελφός to keep this sense of "fellow Jew": Exodus 2.11 and 4.18, Deuteronomy 15.3, 15.12, 17.15, and 18.15. 3 John 9 is apparently the first record of Replacement Theology, a Greek displacing Jewish believers.

3.   "That adherence to the commands of Torah constituted the divine will for Israel appears to have been a conviction held by all pious Jews of the Second Temple Period. It does not follow, however, that Jews believed they were 'earning' their 'salvation' by the 'good works' they performed in keeping the law. Such a notion, **based largely on a misreading of the Pauline evidence and widespread among Christian scholars,** has been attacked in the works of E.P. Sanders. In a study of early rabbinic materials, the DSS and the (OT) Apocrypha and Pseudepigrapha, Sanders concluded that 'covenantal nomism' is characteristic of virtually the whole of literature: i.e., Israel's standing before God is not perceived as 'earned' by human obedience, but as based on the divine election of Israel as His covenantal people; obedience to the laws of Torah was regarded as necessary if the Israelite's position in the covenant was to be maintained, but such obedience was a response to God's grace rather than the means by which salvation was earned." [Emphasis added] General Editor

Geoffrey W. Bromiley, *The International Standard Bible Encyclopedia* (Grand Rapids, MI: William B. Eerdmans Publishing Company, 1979) Torah, Vol. 4, p. 878. This is exactly the same attitude toward faith, salvation, and Law among most Torah-seekers today. Keeping Torah follows salvation, a response of obedience. The believer in Yeshua has the additional assurance, "If we confess our sins, he is faithful and just to forgive us our sins, and to cleanse us from all unrighteousness," 1 John 1.9.

4.   Exodus 20.8-11, "Remember the sabbath day, to keep it holy. Six days shalt thou labour, and do all thy work: But the seventh day *is* the sabbath of the LORD thy God: *in it* thou shalt not do any work, thou, nor thy son, nor thy daughter, thy manservant, nor thy maidservant, nor thy cattle, nor thy stranger that *is* within thy gates: For *in* six days the LORD made heaven and earth, the sea, and all that in them *is*, and rested the seventh day: wherefore the LORD blessed the sabbath day, and hallowed it." **See Thesis 83.**

5.   "Now the Scriptures alone do not contain all the truths which a Christian is bound to believe, nor do they explicitly enjoin all the duties which he is obliged to practice. Not to mention other examples, is not every Christian obliged to sanctify Sunday and to abstain on that day from unnecessary servile work? Is not the observance of this law among the most prominent of our sacred duties? But you may read the Bible from Genesis to Revelation, and you will not find a single line authorizing the sanctification of Sunday. The Scriptures enforce the religious observance of Saturday, a day which we never sanctify." James Gibbons, Cardinal Archbishop of Baltimore, *The Faith of Our Fathers* (Baltimore, MD, New York: John Murphy Company, Ninety-third edition 1917, originally published 1876) Chapter 8, The Church and the Bible, p. 89.

6.   "On the venerable day of the Sun let the magistrates and people residing in cities rest, and let all workshops be closed." Philip Schaff, *History of the Christian Church: Vol. III.* (New York: Charles Scribner's Sons, 1884) page 380, note 1.

7.   Exodus 31.12-17. Verse 16 uses the phrase, בְּרִית עוֹלָם *b'rit olam* perpetual covenant: "Wherefore the children of

Israel shall keep the sabbath, to observe the sabbath throughout their generations, *for* a perpetual covenant." B'rit olam is also the expression in Genesis 9.16. By the rainbow, God promises never again to destroy the earth with water. See Thesis 14.

8.	Catholic Encyclopedia, article on Johann Tetzel, http://www.catholic.org/encyclopedia/view.php?id=11398 Accessed July 23, 2014.

9.	Martin Luther, *Martin Luther's Basic Theological Writings, Third Edition* (Minneapolis, MN: Fortress Press e-book, 2012) Chapter 2, *The Ninety-Five Theses* (1517) p. 15 of 505.

10.	ibid., Chapter 32, *Smalcald Articles II* (1537) p. 391 of 505.

11.	ibid., Chapter 14, *How Christians Should Regard Moses* (1525), p. 109 of 505.

12.	1 Corinthians 10.1-13.

13.	Mark Twain, *The Innocents Abroad* (New York: Penguin Books, 2002) pp. 365, 463.

14.	Jeremiah 31.35-37, "Thus saith the LORD, which giveth the sun for a light by day, *and* the ordinances of the moon and of the stars for a light by night, which divideth the sea when the waves thereof roar; The LORD of hosts *is* his name: If those ordinances depart from before me, saith the LORD, *then* the seed of Israel also shall cease from being a nation before me for ever. Thus saith the LORD; If heaven above can be measured, and the foundations of the earth searched out beneath, I will also cast off all the seed of Israel for all that they have done, saith the LORD."

15.	Matthew 5.17-18, "Think not that I am come to destroy the **Torah**, or the prophets: I am not come to destroy, but to fulfil. For verily I say unto you, Till heaven and earth pass, one jot or one tittle shall in no wise pass from the **Torah**, till all be fulfilled."

16.	Ezekiel 36.33-35, "Thus saith the Lord GOD; In the day that I shall have cleansed *you* from all your iniquities I will also cause you to dwell in the cities, and the wastes shall be builded. And the desolate land shall be tilled, whereas it lay desolate in the sight of all that passed by. And they shall say, This land that was desolate is become like the garden of Eden; and the waste and desolate and ruined cities *are become* fenced, *and* are inhabited." Ezekiel 37.5, 9b-10, "Thus saith the Lord GOD unto these bones; Behold, I will cause breath to enter into you, and ye shall live…Come from the four winds, O breath, and breathe upon these slain, that they may live. So I prophesied as he commanded me, and the breath came into them, and they lived, and stood up upon their feet, an exceeding great army." Verse 14, "And shall put my spirit in you, and ye shall live, and I shall place you in your own land: then shall ye know that I the LORD have spoken *it*, and performed *it*, saith the LORD." The first fulfillment of Ezekiel's prophecies was Israel's return from Babylon. But after a much greater exile for almost 2,000 years, we now see a much greater return. The cities are bigger and the army far more powerful than at any other time. The order is revealing: after the establishment of the cities and the army with רוּחַ *ruach* breath from the four winds (v. 9), God then gives them His רוּחַ *ruach* Spirit (v. 14). So for those who consider Israel to be only a secular nation today, these verses do not preclude what we see happening as a fulfillment of this prophecy, with God yet to fill Israel with His Holy Spirit.

17.   Exodus 32.14, "And the LORD repented of the evil which he thought to do unto his people."

18.   Eusebius Pamphilus, *The Life of the Blessed Emperor Constantine, in Four Books, from 306 to 337 AD* (London: Samuel Bagster and Sons, 1845) Book III, Chapter XVIII, p. 129.

19.   *Yale Law School's Avalon Project, Nuremberg Trial Proceedings* (http://avalon.law.yale.edu/imt/04-29-46.asp accessed July 24, 2014) Vol. 12, One Hundred and Sixteenth Day, Monday, 29 April 1946, Morning Session, p. 318.

20.   "First…Moses writes in Deuteronomy that where a city practiced idolatry, it should be entirely destroyed with fire and leave nothing. If he were living today he would be the first to put fire to the Jew schools and houses… Secondly, that you also refuse to let them own houses among us… Thirdly, that you take away from them all of their prayer books and Talmuds wherein such lying, cursing, and blaspheming is taught.

Fourthly, that you prohibit their rabbis to teach… Fifthly, that protection for Jews on highways be revoked. For they have no right to be in the land, because they are not lords, nor officials. They should stay at home… Sixthly, that their usury be prohibited, which was prohibited by Moses, where they are not lords in their own country over strange lands, and take away all the currency and silver and gold and put it away for safekeeping… Finally: That young, strong Jews be given the flail, ax, spade, spindle, and let them earn their bread in the sweat of their noses as imposed upon Adam's children…" Martin Luther, *The Jews and Their Lies* (York, SC: Liberty Bell Publications, Reprinted 2004) pp. 37-43.

21.	In 1994, the Church Council of the Evangelical Lutheran Church in America (ELCA) rejected Luther's anti-Semitic writings. Many other Lutheran denominations have done likewise.

22.	"The Fuhrer made it known to those entrusted with the Final Solution that the killings should be done as humanely as possible. This was in line with his conviction that he was observing God's injunction to cleanse the world of vermin. Still a member in good standing of the Church of Rome despite detestation of its hierarchy ('I am now as before a Catholic and will always remain so'), he carried within him its teaching that the Jew was the killer of God. The extermination, therefore, could be done without a twinge of conscience since he was merely acting as the avenging hand of God—so long as it was done impersonally, without cruelty." John Toland, *Adolf Hitler* (New York: Ballantine Books, 1976) p. 503.

23.	Deuteronomy 13.1-5, "If there arise among you a prophet, or a dreamer of dreams, and giveth thee a sign or a wonder, And the sign or the wonder come to pass, whereof he spake unto thee, saying, Let us go after other gods, which thou hast not known, and let us serve them; Thou shalt not hearken unto the words of that prophet, or that dreamer of dreams: for the LORD your God proveth you, to know whether ye love the LORD your God with all your heart and with all your soul. Ye shall walk after the LORD your God, and fear him, and keep his commandmdents, and obey his voice, and ye shall serve him, and cleave unto him. And that prophet, or that dreamer of dreams, shall be put to death; because he hath spoken to turn *you* away from the LORD your God, which brought you out of the land of Egypt, and redeemed you out of the house of bondage, to thrust thee out of the way which the LORD thy God commanded thee to walk in. So shalt thou put the evil away from the midst of thee."

24.   Acts 17.10-11, "And the brethren immediately sent away Paul and Silas by night unto Berea: who coming *thither* went into the synagogue of the Jews. These were more noble than those in Thessalonica, in that they received the word with all readiness of mind, and searched the scriptures daily, whether those things were so."

25.   Revelation 12.17, "And the dragon was wroth with the woman, and went to make war with the remnant of her seed, which keep the commandments of God, and have the testimony of Jesus Christ." **Revelation 14.12,** "Here is the patience of the saints: here *are* they that keep the commandments of God, and the faith of Jesus."

26.   According to Masorite scribes, the middle words of Torah are Leviticus 10.16a, וְאֵת שְׂעִיר הַחַטָּאת דָּרֹשׁ דָּרַשׁ מֹשֶׁה *ve-et se-ir ha-cha-tat da-rosh da-rash Mo-she,* "And Moses diligently sought the goat of the sin offering." Each דָּרַשׁ *darash* seek falls in separate halves of Torah. Jesus Cordero, "Yeshua the Lamb," of 99designs.com designed this book's cover.

27.   2 Corinthians 5.21, "For he hath made him *to be* sin for us, who knew no sin; that we might be made the righteousness of God in him." The first sin offering for the congregation of Israel, in the first Tabernacle, with the first fire from God, wasn't completed, Leviticus 10.16-20. Hebrews 9.11-12 says that Yeshua offered his own blood in heaven's Holy Place. Yeshua by his death and resurrection fulfilled the sin offering for the congregation of Israel.

28.   John 5.46-47, "For had ye believed Moses, ye would have believed me: for he wrote of me. But if ye believe not his writings, how shall ye believe my words?"

29.   Matthew 15.21-28, "Then Jesus went thence, and departed into the coasts of Tyre and Sidon. And, behold, a woman of Canaan came out of the same coasts, and cried unto him, saying, Have mercy on me, O Lord, *thou* Son of David; my daughter is grievously vexed with a devil. But he answered her not a word. And his disciples came and besought him, saying, Send her away; for she crieth after us. But he answered and said, I am not sent but unto the lost sheep of the house of Israel. Then came she and worshipped him, saying, Lord, help me. But he answered and said, It is not meet to take the children's bread, and to cast *it* to dogs. And she said, Truth, Lord: yet the dogs eat of the crumbs which fall from their masters' table. Then Jesus answered and said unto her, O woman, great *is* thy faith: be it unto thee even as thou wilt. And her daughter was made whole from that very hour."

30.   Psalm 40.8. See Thesis 18.

31.   The Greek name Ἰησοῦς *Iēsous* Jesus, G2424, means God is Salvation, from יְהוֹשׁוּעַ *Yĕhowshuwa* Joshua, H3091. Moses' aide Joshua was the Son of Nun. In Nehemiah 8.17, Joshua's name is shortened to יֵשׁוּעַ *Yeshuwa*, H3442. Yeshua is a shortened version of Joshua, sharing the root יָשַׁע *yasha* to save. Both lead us to the Promised Land through faith followed by lives of Torah obedience.

32.   Maimonides, *Mishneh Torah*, translated by Eliyahu Touger (http://www.chabad.org/library/article_cdo/aid/1188356/jewish/Melachim-uMilchamot-Chapter-11.htm accessed 09-17-2004) *Melachim uMilchamot*, Chapter 11, Halacha 4.

Chapter 1

1.   Psalm 1.2, Genesis 32.24, Exodus 12.29, Joshua 1.8, Judges 7.19, Judges 16.3, Ruth 3.8, 1 Kings 3.20, Nehemiah 1.6, Nehemiah 4.9, Matthew 2.14, Luke 2.8, Luke 2.37, John 3.19-20, Luke 6.12, Matthew 14.25, Matthew 26.36-56, Luke 22.53, Acts 16.25-26, Acts 27.27-44, Luke 18.7, Matthew 25.6, 1 Thessalonians 5.2, Revelation 4.8.

2.   Dietrich Bonhoeffer, *The Cost of Discipleship* (New York: Simon and Shuster/Touchstone, 1995) p. 48.

Chapter 2

1.   Exodus 12.1-2, "And the LORD spake unto Moses and Aaron in the land of Egypt, saying, This month *shall be* unto you the beginning of months: it *shall be* the first month of the year to you."

2.   "CHAPTER XVIII. [EMPEROR CONSTANTINE] SPEAKS OF THEIR UNANIMITY RESPECTING THE FEAST OF EASTER, AND AGAINST THE PRACTICE OF THE JEWS 'At this meeting the question concerning the most holy day of Easter was discussed, and it was resolved by the united judgment of all present, that this feast ought to be kept by all and in every place on one and the same day. For what can be more becoming or honourable to us than that this feast, from which we date our hopes of immortality, should be observed unfailingly by all alike, according to one ascertained order and arrangement? And first of all, it appeared an unworthy thing that in the celebration of this most holy feast we should follow the practice of the Jews, who have impiously defiled their hands with enormous sin, and are therefore deservedly afflicted with blindness of soul...Hence it is that on this point as well as others they have no perception of the truth, so that, being altogether ignorant of the true adjustment of this question, they sometimes celebrate Easter twice in the same year. Why then should we follow those who are confessedly in grievous error? Surely we shall never consent to keep this feast a second time in the same year...For our Saviour has left us one feast in commemoration of the day of our deliverance, I mean the day of His most holy passion; and He has willed that His Catholic Church should be one, the members of which, however scattered in many and diverse places, are yet cherished by one pervading spirit, that is, by the will of God...It is, then, plainly the will of Divine Providence (as I suppose you all clearly see), that this usage should receive fitting correction, and be reduced to one uniform rule.'" Eusebius Pamphilus, *The Life of the Blessed Emperor Constantine, in Four Books, from 306 to 337 AD* (London: Samuel Bagster and Sons, 1845) Book III, Chapter XVIII, pp.

128-131. Note that Emperor Constantine contradicted Torah three times. By submitting to his authority, the church strayed further from God's Word. First, he says that the church shouldn't follow the practice of the Jews in setting the date, when actually Torah sets the date. By rejecting Jews, the church rejected Torah. Second, by saying that the Jews "sometimes celebrate Easter twice in the same year," he equates Easter, a manmade feast, with Passover, a strictly biblical remembrance of God rescuing Israel from Egypt. Passover is the event which forms the basis for the covenant relationship between God and His people: "And God spake all these words, saying, I am the LORD thy God, which have brought thee out of the land of Egypt, out of the house of bondage. Thou shalt have no other gods before me," Exodus 20.1-3, the beginning of the Ten Commandments. See Thesis 80. Third, by the same quote, Constantine expresses ignorance of Torah, which allowed for two dates for Passover. The first date is in the first month, Nisan 14, and the second allowable date is the fourteenth of the second month. This second date could be necessitated by a person being ritually unclean through contact with the dead on the first date, and allows the person to keep Passover after the period of cleansing. The error belonged to Constantine and the church, not Torah and the Jews. Numbers 9.5-14, "And they kept the passover on the fourteenth day of the first month at even in the wilderness of Sinai: according to all that the LORD commanded Moses, so did the children of Israel. And there were certain men, who were defiled by the dead body of a man, that they could not keep the passover on that day: and they came before Moses and before Aaron on that day: And those men said unto him, We *are* defiled by the dead body of a man: wherefore are we kept back, that we may not offer an offering of the LORD in his appointed season among the children of Israel? And Moses said unto them, Stand still, and I will hear what the LORD will command concerning you. And the LORD spake unto Moses, saying, Speak unto the children of Israel, saying, If any man of you or of your posterity shall be unclean by reason of a dead body, or *be* in a journey afar off, yet he shall keep the passover unto the LORD. The fourteenth day of the second month at even they shall keep it, *and* eat it with unleavened bread and bitter *herbs*. They shall leave none of it unto the morning, nor break any bone of it: according to all the ordinances of the passover they shall keep it. But the man that *is* clean, and is not in a journey, and forbeareth to keep the passover, even the same soul shall be cut off from among his people: because he brought not the offering of the LORD in his appointed season, that man shall bear his sin. And if a stranger shall sojourn among you, and will keep the passover unto the LORD; according to the ordinance of the passover, and according to the manner thereof, so shall he do: ye shall have one ordinance, both for the stranger, and for him that was born in the land." Torah allowed certain Gentiles to celebrate Passover with Israel. It was not necessary for the church to turn a preexisting pagan feast into a church event. That's what happened at the sin of the Golden Calf, Exodus 32.

3. Middle East Media Research Institute (MEMRI) www.memri.org Clip #1784, June 2, 2008, (http://www.memritv.org/clip_transcript/en/1784.htm. accessed September 1, 2014)

4. Judah ben Samuel, translated from the original German by Ludwig Schneider, *Israel Today* (Israel, March 2008) p. 18.

Chapter 3

1. Geoffrey W. Bromiley, General Editor, International Standard Bible Encyclopedia (Grand Rapids: William B. Eerdmans Publishing Company, 1979) Galatia, Volume II, p. 378.

2. ibid., Hostility, Dividing Wall of, Volume II, p. 768.

3. Kenneth Barker, General Editor, *The NIV Study Bible* (Grand Rapids, Michigan: Zondervan Publishing House, 1985) p. 1793.

4. Christian Research Institute, Bible Answer Man broadcast, March 20, 2015, beginning at 21 minutes into the show (http://www.equip.org/category/broadcasts/page/2/ accessed April 2, 2015.)

Chapter 5

The Four Steps

1.   Matthew 18.15-17, "Moreover if thy brother shall trespass against thee, go and tell him his fault between thee and him alone: if he shall hear thee, thou hast gained thy brother. But if he will not hear *thee, then* take with thee one or two more, that in the mouth of two or three witnesses every word may be established. And if he shall neglect to hear them, tell *it* unto the church: but if he neglect to hear the church, let him be unto thee as an heathen man and a publican."

    1.   When you have a conflict with a fellow believer, go to your brother or sister privately. That is first. Privacy protects dignity.

    2.   If your brother or sister won't listen, take one or two others along to make your case. If you can't get anyone to agree with you, you may be wrong.

    3.   If he or she still won't listen, take it to the church.

    4.   If he or she won't listen to the church, treat him or her as a pagan and a tax collector.